Launched in 1986, *Q Magazine* remained the UK's leading contemporary monthly music publication, until its closure in 2020.

THE 10 COMMANDMENTS

THE ROCK STAR'S GUIDE TO LIFE
FROM THE MAKERS OF *Q MAGAZINE*

Edited by Ted Kessler

corsair

CORSAIR

First published in Great Britain in 2018 by Corsair
This paperback edition published in 2020

1 3 5 7 9 10 8 6 4 2

Copyright © Q Magazine, 2018

A CIP catalogue record for this book
is available from the British Library.

ISBN: 978-1-4721-5575-7

Printed and bound in Great Britain by Clays Ltd, Elcograf S.p.A.

Papers used by Corsair are from well-managed forests
and other responsible sources.

Corsair
An imprint of
Little, Brown Book Group
Carmelite House
50 Victoria Embankment
London EC4Y 0DZ

An Hachette UK Company
www.hachette.co.uk

www.littlebrown.co.uk

Introduction
from the Editor

Noel Gallagher famously sang that listeners of Oasis should not put their 'life in the hands of a rock and roll band'. I disagree.

Everything good in my life was recommended to me by my musical heroes. My moral compass has been set more or less entirely by pop stars. No teacher, no institution, no writer (ok, maybe some writers, actually) has had the same impact upon me as rock stars. Who forged your direction in life? Your parents? School? Your peers? Maybe it was a religious calling, or even a political party. Or maybe because you're reading this book, you're still searching for illumination. You've come to the right place.

I drew everything I believe in, initially, from Paul Weller, lead singer with The Jam. He changed my life, forever. The London I grew up in the late 1970s was grim: the rubbish piled up, the National Front daubed their initials upon school walls, Thatcher snatched our milk. But Weller rocked up with visions of social utopia attached to the kind of chorus that any idiot 11-year-old could remember. His clothes were fantastic. He was

pictured reading Alan Sillitoe and George Orwell. He pro-
claimed that his fans should investigate an array of soul, reggae,
funk and '6os beat records. He signed off his fan letters with
the advice that we should 'stay cool, clean and hard'. I soaked
it all up and his maxims became the foundations upon which
the rest of my life was built. I still dress a bit like he did in 1983.

Other great teachers followed: Kevin Rowland, Mark E
Smith, Siouxsie, Chuck D, Lou Reed, Patti Smith, Beastie
Boys ... All with their own distinct philosophies, experiences
and influences, and all available to download directly into the
brain via their music and, especially, their interviews, which
I devoured.

And so, as editor of the UK's greatest music magazine, Q,
I've always been drawn to methods that can deliver the lessons
that have been learnt by rock stars most directly to the readers.
10 Commandments, which is a spread Q has run for around a
decade in which stars from across the generational spectrum
of music deliver their life lessons, is easily the most profoundly
enjoyable, and enjoyably profound, method for this.

Skip through the pages of this book and stop at a page at
random. What we do learn? Let's see. Ezra Koenig, frontman with Vampire Weekend suggests that you DO YOUR
EMAILS WHILE YOU DRINK YOUR COFFEE. Why?
Well, imbued with caffeine-enhanced empathy 'you are presenting the best version of yourself.' Reader, I do this now and
it's true. Take another flick through the book ... and stop.
Oh, Neneh Cherry. What does she recommend? EMBRACE
THE AGEING PROCESS. 'I can't change getting older.' Very
true, enjoy the here and now. And who's this, on page 215? Noel
Gallagher, of course. What are his words of wisdom? DON'T

ALWAYS TRUST PAUL WELLER'S TASTE. Yes, well, let's skip over that one exception that proves all the other rules . . .

The 10 Commandments is packed with lots of brand new interviews, as well as some of our old favourites. All are deeply illuminating. I'd advise keeping your copy close at hand even after you've read it, for those moments when ennui or dilemma bites deep. It'll help you navigate crises, it'll provide inspiration. Place it on a lower shelf, too, if possible. You never know when any children in your home will need to have their lives rearranged for the better by it.

Ted Kessler, Editor, *Q Magazine*, 2018.

Contents

THE 10 COMMANDMENTS

Shirley Manson

Singer, Garbage

'Being young is torturous. Getting older taught me how to live'

ENGINEER YOUR OWN HAPPINESS

When I was most successful I was never more miserable. I had everything I thought I wanted and it didn't make me feel good in any way. When attention and success fell away I had to engineer a lovely life, independent of external validation. Find small things that make you happy – a great cup of coffee, meditation, walking the dog, dancing – and inject them into your life. What's the secret to a great coffee? I don't know but I married a man who does. Little things that can be prepared to be enjoyed are priceless.

BE AUTHENTIC

The most interesting version of you is the truthful one. It's unique – with all the flaws. You can't have a good life if you're telling lies to please others. You get trapped by the lies. As you get older you can't find the energy to lie and the real you comes spilling out.

BE A FEMINIST

Be one if you're a woman, and if you're a man too. Until the sexes are evenly balanced we are all operating at a disadvantage. Women won't ever enjoy equality without help from our male counterparts. They may question why they want to support that but a happy queen leads to a happy king. But a happy king without a happy queen is not a good scene.

DON'T BE A GOOD GIRL

There seems to be increasing pressure on women to look a certain way, act a certain way, be a certain way. I say, fuck it. Be whoever you want to be. Write your own rules. Fuck the system: it's designed to watch you fail.

ALWAYS SPEAK UP

Far too much is made of keeping your opinions to yourself. A healthy culture comes from debate and tolerating different opinions. I don't want to be a passive participant in my life, I want to be an active one. I want to stand up against injustice rather than be quietly outraged from afar. I don't think that's helping anybody.

GO PLACES

Travel and garner different perspectives. Learning from other cultures has been a formidable force. Going to Bhutan where they prize happiness over everything else blew my brains. And seeing the poverty in India – orphaned children living on a traffic island – put everything in perspective. When I hear people moan about their lot I think, 'Be grateful you're not growing up on a traffic island! Shut the fuck up [laughs]!'

READ MORE

A love of books has brought me incredible comfort over the years. No matter how difficult life can get, you can escape into a book, into another person's story and be transported out of your reality. It's expanded my world view. It's just a love of words, language, the means by which we can all communicate and connect. Connection is important to me. I want to be connected and not just a voyeur on the outskirts, I want to be invested in my life.

LIFE IS SHORT BUT STORIES ARE LONG

When I was young I compared myself to others, feeling like other people had more than I did. I came to realise stories are not set in stone. You are continually evolving. Even when things seem bleak and there's no way out, you don't know how things will end. So don't give up on yourself. Every single minute of the day you change and your circumstances change and what can seem dark in the evening can be completely different in the morning.

LIVE IN THE PRESENT

I used to really concern myself with the past and my own darkness. I have no floor to my darkness, I could examine it forever. As I got older, I became aware of my mortality. I might die tomorrow so let's make now as pleasant as possible. Getting older has been nothing but pleasant: I feel so much better as a human. When I was young I felt so unhappy, uncomfortable, unsafe and uncertain. I don't know why everyone harps on about how great it is to be young, 'cos it's actually torturous. Getting older taught me how to live.

LISTEN TO VINYL

A few years ago a flood destroyed my entire vinyl collection. My heart was broken. Then for my birthday last year I got a turntable and reinvested in my record collection. It's brought me so much pleasure. Really listening to a record is magical. I've encouraged my friends to do the same and we have Vinyl Nights. It's life-enhancing, a meditation of sorts.

Rod Stewart

Singer

'I'll tell you who's a good footballer, Tubs. The Take That guy? Robbie! He's good. Tubs, I call him'

STUDY THE GREATS

I used to listen to Sam Cooke, Muddy Waters, all the greats over and over again just trying to roughen my voice up. If you hear my first ever recording, a thing called 'Good Morning Little Schoolgirl' by Muddy Waters, there's hardly any gravel there at all. You couldn't get away with a title like that nowadays. 'Good morning little schoolgirl, can I come home with you?' Are you serious?!? Fuck!

PAY YOUR DUES

It's what I call the apprenticeship. You learn the art of engaging the audience, which I don't think *The X Factor* can teach you. I'm actually for *The X Factor* but the downside of it is the psychological impact of someone being so close to success and then suddenly it's turned off. That's it, you're forgotten about, you're back sleeping in your mum's spare room. When we started, fame and fortune were the last things we thought of. We just wanted to do this because it felt good. It was like wanking, I suppose.

LADIES STILL LOVE A FRONTMAN

Being a singer in a band you could really pull the birds; it didn't matter what you looked like. If you were the singer in a band, mate, that was pretty powerful stuff. It still is! You always get the first choice of the girls.

NOT ALL POP STARS CAN PLAY FOOTBALL

When I had [Stewart's expat football team in LA] The Exiles, and other musicians would come for a kick about with us, there weren't many good ones, I must admit. One I can remember who wasn't very good – although he thought he was good – was Mick Hucknall. He was a good trier. I'll tell you who is a good player, Tubs. What's his name? The Take That guy? Robbie! Robbie's a good player. Tubs, I call him. He's useful.

SONGWRITING AIN'T EASY

I never did like songwriting. It was always a bit of a struggle because I'd have to stay at home and write the lyrics while everyone was out a-shagging and a-drinking. But now it's an absolute joy – I don't know whether that's just come with age or whatever.

DON'T DRINK PORT ON AN EMPTY STOMACH

In The Faces we never got drunk just for the sake of getting drunk. We would all be in the dressing room passing round a bottle of Mateus Rosé, then we'd go out and play. We had the barman onstage, he had a proper bar and would bring us drinks on a tray. When Kenney [Jones] had his drum solo on (I Know) I'm Losing You, we'd all go to the bar and [sticks elbow out] watch him. 'You carry on, we'll just have a quick one!' Our decline when it came to alcohol consumption was when one of us decided to start drinking port and brandy on an empty stomach. There was an agreement: 'Let's have a big breakfast, skip lunch, then have a port and brandy tonight and it will REALLY get us going.' There were some serious hangovers ...

YOU DON'T HAVE TO SPEND A
PACKET TO LOOK SMART

I've always loved clothes. I love [Spanish high street chain] Zara. I went into the one in Rio in Brazil and bought four pairs of trousers, three shirts and a couple of jackets – 220 bucks. My son, right, he goes down to Ralph Lauren and buys a pair of shoes for 600 bucks. I say, 'Go to Zara, what's wrong with you?' I've got a load of Topman stuff, too. There's nothing wrong with the high street at all. I haven't been into Dolce & Gabbana for donkey's years.

SLOPPY IS GOOD

When The Faces played together again it wasn't the same, but the spirit was there, that sloppiness. Now Ronnie Lane's gone we can't blame it on him, there's only three of us left. I had to stop one of the songs at one point. I said, 'Ronnie [Wood], we can't play this song, it's well out of time, we'll have to start again.' He said, 'I'll start it again, Rod, but it's gonna be the same!'

DOWNTON ABBEY, YES, BAKE OFF, NO

It does suck you in, doesn't it? I've got no guilt about it but I do love *Downton Abbey*. Lady Mary [Downton actress Michelle Dockery] came to The Faces concert in Surrey, which I was pleased about. Do I watch *The Great British Bake Off*? No, you've got to draw the line somewhere, mate.

SOMETIMES YOU HAVE TO MAKE A CHOICE

I only finished playing football about a year and a half ago. I was playing in an over-50s league and was getting too old! I can't describe how much I miss it. I was playing on Sunday mornings in LA and the pitches out there are fucking awful. That was my demise, really, because the old knee was killing me. I'd play half a game, then my knee would start hurting and I'd have to hobble on at Caesars Palace in the evening, so one of the two had to go!

Tori Amos

Singer

*'The sexiest thing about a man is
when he looks after his family'*

BE A SURVIVOR, NOT A VICTIM

My great-great grandmother was Eastern Cherokee and a
real template for me. At 16, she survived the round-up [19th-
century genocide of native Americans] by hiding in the Smoky
Mountains for nine months. When the Civil War broke out
and the soldiers burnt everything, farms, oxen, she planted
seeds in Christian graves because she knew the Christian soldiers wouldn't violate their own graves. She became the oxen
[farming the soil on the graves] and so survived. You can either
be part of Victims Anonymous or Survivors Anonymous.

DON'T BOTHER WITH DIGITAL CENSORSHIP

I live in a world of parchment so I learn about the digital world from my daughter, Tash [Natashya, 13]. We don't have limits or censorship, but she's on her dad's iTunes account so he knows. And she knows he knows. So there's no need to sneak. Parameters just make the bad things more attractive anyway.

YOU DON'T HAVE TO STRIP OFF

When I was coming up in the early '90s with Björk and Polly [PJ Harvey] it wasn't cool to be overtly sexual. Now, everyone's taking their clothes off. Is it down to executives or is it also cultural demand? I look at this through Tash's eyes and she can like someone's music but not be seduced by the image they're pushing. She loves Audrey Hepburn and you didn't see a lot of flesh from her.

CHERISH ROMANCE

I believe in romance. There's a lot of desire out there but what about really falling in love with somebody? Not just someone thinking you're hot, someone who wants to walk in the rain with you and hold your hand. Really fancying someone because of the way they think. I've been married for 16 years and fell more in love with my husband in the last few months than ever before. You can fall in love again and again with your mate.

IF YOU'RE IN THE DESERT, LOOK
AFTER THE MAYONNAISE

I used to camp out in the Joshua Tree [National Park] with friends and the rule was, 'Make sure your cold boxes are cold.' In the desert anything can get ruined, especially anything with mayonnaise. One of the things I do better in life is make sandwiches. The sandwich would be roast chicken, on toasted seeded grain, with Jarlsberg, rocket, tomato, spring onions and a mayo-mustard mix. I've worked on it for many years.

A SEXY MAN IS ONE WHO
LOOKS AFTER HIS FAMILY

The sexiest thing about a man is when he looks after his family. When he's there for them, is compassionate, isn't critical. That's enough to make a woman fall in love with a man. And if she doesn't fall in love with a guy for those qualities, she isn't worthy, so move on!

DON'T SMASH UP YOUR
INSTRUMENTS ANY MORE

A long time ago people smashed up their instruments but with the music business in the state it's in? Before you smash one up, give it to a starving musician. Setting fire to a piano might have been done before but a [pricey Austrian piano brand] Bösendorfer? It's worth more than some people's houses!

FIND THE RIGHT KIND OF BADASS

I speak to girls in their 20s who say, 'I like bad boys' and I say, 'You need to redefine bad boy.' If a guy demeans you and needs to belittle you, if he needs to control you, that's abuse. A 'badass' is a man who adores his woman, makes her feel good about herself. Those guys are on my altar.

FIND A GOOD ACCOUNTANT

If you're a touring entity, track down accountants who understand international tax laws. And when someone says, 'I know what I'm doing' – no, don't ever take anybody's word for that, you need to see the qualifications. Proof!

SUPPORT THE SISTERHOOD

The music and entertainment business pits women against each other. It's really important we're not negative about our sisters, but supportive. It's women who are critical of women. It's almost as if we find success when another woman faces failure or public ridicule. If another woman doesn't get that promotion or her partner left her for a younger woman, the little green monster says, 'Finally she's going to be like the rest of us.' Well, that's not a very good place to be, is it!?

Bono

(*Eleven Commandments – he *had* to be different)

Singer, U2

> '*We needed more rules. Thou shalt not*
> *wear a mullet for a start. A rock star*
> *should not look like his hair is ironed*'

> '*Larry Mullen Jr looked deeply into my eyes and*
> *said, "Bono, question everything." I said, "Why?"*'

THOU SHALT BELIEVE IN THE BLANK PAGE

Everybody has one. Cos everybody is one. Fill it up. Tear it up. Let it tear you up. A blank page threatens the author with emptiness, but that's OK. Believe in it and believe you can make your mark on it. It's your future. Your only hope. It's the place you need to be. Move in. Have faith in the blank page. It can be anything, and it is the only thing that can truly save your life. That's what I now know Richard Hell was talking about in *Blank Generation* years ago. It's possibility. The poet spoke the truth. As I'm sure he knew he must.

QUESTION EVERYTHING.

Like many things, I learned this from the band oracle Larry Mullen Jr. He took me aside after a gig and told me he needed to tell me something extremely important. He took my hand. Looked deeply into my eyes, and said, 'Bono, question everything.' I said, 'Why?'

WHAT'S GREAT

Will wait.
  But not forever.

WHEN ACCUSED OF GENIUS, GENEROUSLY AND HUMBLY CONFESS

Be quick to do it for fear of further accusations of tardiness, lethargy or humility. A self-confessed genius is a great thing, and there are far too few of them in this world, though perhaps a few too many on the Northside of Dublin, currently speaking, where being backwards about being forward is an unknown performance so far.

THE BEST U2 ALBUM IS ALWAYS THE
ONE WE'RE WORKING ON

Because the music of what is, is fine music. But the music of what might be, is finer still. Still searching for the crock of gold. The journey is the destination, etc., etc. Get out there and enjoy your football ...

A SINGLE TRANSFERABLE PHRASE IS
AN ESSENTIAL AND HANDY TOOL

That I don't possess. In any situation, whether being harangued, bored, seduced, abused or adored, it would be helpful. I complained about this to Jarvis Cocker who understood the problem at the molecular level and offered, without missing a beat, 'It's a lot to take in, really.' He explained that this STP always cooled folks down or at least put them on a pause – whatever they were on about. Lemmy, while musing pleasantly on this and that, be it the injustice of the world, the horrors of war, or the perfidy of a man's love for women, would shrug and say, 'Oh, well, you can't have everything, where would you put it?' A phrase that works on every occasion is an invaluable exit strategy. I need one. However, when speaking to Q scribes, beware the pithy quote out of context. I just did a one-and-a-half-hour briefing with the United States Senate on the refugee crisis. Off-script, in the last five minutes, I made one joke about sending Amy Schumer, Sacha Baron Cohen and Chris Rock in to fight ISIS and that's all that ended up on the news. I guess people don't want me to be funny ...

THOU SHALT BELIEVE IN TWO THINGS AT THE SAME TIME

Though I'm not sure about this one.

THOU SHALT NOT PLAY GOLF

Limitation leads to innovation and a rule book is useful even if you eventually tear it up. U2 had musical notes we wouldn't use (certain bendy ones from a blues scale on guitar) and lyrics we decided were against the law like BABY and CRAZY. It took 20 years but we eventually loosened up on both and included the forbidden 'baby' in the title of our seventh album and had it appear 23 times in the music. In truth, we needed more rules. Thou shalt not wear a mullet for a start, a rock star should not look like his hair is ironed. Thou shalt not play golf is another. When we started as a band we committed to the principles of a golf-free band. Many mistakes were allowed for some of us who did terrible things that deserved firing but nobody ever played golf. Except, we think, The Edge.

IT'S NOT ABOUT THE MONEY, IT'S THE MONEY

There are more than a couple of reasons to get the money right, but let's start with the fact that it's the number one reason bands break up. Not musical differences, it's money differences. The songwriting, how it's shared, who did what when and why that song was left off, etc., etc. If you're the only one in the band who writes, remember the thing that will make your song famous is the band's playing of it. In U2 we decided to split things equally. I think it's at the top of the list of reasons we've lasted so long. Also, do the math or make sure you have somebody numerate to do it for you. Pay attention to business, it's really a drag when it goes wrong. Adam Clayton, normally so fastidious about his friends, his art, his style, can fill you in on what can happen when you're too preoccupied with beauty ... ugly stuff. Just because you're smart with your art or your activism doesn't mean you have to be dumb with your money.

THOU SHALT NOT BREAK UP THE BAND

As Joe Strummer screamed, 'Break the law but don't break up the band!!!!' There's nothing more arduous but nothing more fun than a band. I've met only one person who left a great band and told me that life was better having rid the room of argument ... but, apart from Sting, remember all of you who go solo, that the innate friction of a real band brings out special qualities in your music, as does the acquiescence inherent in for-hire musicians however talented ... it's different, it's a different kind of sound. I know many great records were made on wages but it's not the same ... Why oh why do bands break up (see Commandment 9) ... Note: watch out for answering your own rhetorical questions ... Well, as sure as 14 follows three, in anthropology we discover that the male finds it harder and harder to work around other males as he reaches so-called maturity. So stop trying. Picasso said it takes a long time to become young. This is why a protracted adolescence, a refusal of adulthood is somewhere close to the centre of rock'n'roll. Creativity needs brightly coloured crayons. Believe it or not, my best friend Guggi and I pledged to stay age eight when we were eight and mostly we have succeeded (though I have spotted hair growing on his face and back, and he talks about girls more). As a final subpoint, I would mention it is enviable to have best friends who knew you before you were famous, even better if you can marry one.

NEVER SPEAK ABOUT YOURSELF IN THE THIRD PERSON

Bono hates that.

John Lydon

Singer, Sex Pistols/PiL

'Anarchy seems to be an act of jealousy.
I'd put it with the seven deadly sins'

DON'T LIMIT YOURSELF

My golden rules!? God, where do I begin? Well, my first rule is:
I hate lists that limit my expectations in life!

KEEP RELIGION OUT OF SCHOOLS

In a list of importance, religion comes in at Number 2 because of
all the trouble it's been causing throughout the centuries. I don't
want to see religion taught in schools ever again. Nobody has the
right, whatever their religion, to impose their beliefs on me or
anybody else that thinks differently to them. And, of course, that
leads us down the merry road of a woman's right to choose and
no man has got the right to poke his knob in there you know, he's
done his business now fuck off! It's her who's gotta live with it!

GOVERNMENTS MUST BE TRANSPARENT

I think any government in the modern age that requires any type of secrecy isn't a government at all. It's a kind of backwards dwarfism that is keeping us firmly locked in feudalism, hatred and wars. And it was very fun to watch Bernie Sanders, who seems like a typical Labour MP, sort of like Tony Benn's grubby cousin, having a go at the American system. Jeremy Corbyn is even more extreme and excessive and highly amusing, but impractical. They're like a Students' Union discussion group that's gone too far down a loser, dead end because it's not open-minded and is completely absorbed in the philosophy and dictates of this new religion called politics. That sort of extreme politics is hateful because it's not transparent and offers no solution. It's 'my way or the highway' – well, fuck off both of you!

ALWAYS BE HONEST TO YOUR WIFE

I've been married for 40 years and the secret to a successful marriage is honesty and openness. You have to know each other's thoughts so they become so well aligned that you have respect for each other and there's no need for lies. Commitment is something you shouldn't do lightly, but once you've done it, it's there forever.

BE PREPARED TO PUT YOUR HEAD ON THE BLOCK

Only go into making music if you really, really love it and really want to do it. If your motivation is just wanting to be a 'pop star' then forget it because that's the kiss of death. The other way is hard slog – being prepared to put your head on the chopping block on a daily basis because you will be judged harshly and wrongly almost continuously but in your heart and soul you know you're right.

DON'T BE NOSEY

Social media is a very, very silly thing. I think it's evil the way people anonymously poke their noses into other people's private lives. Who is shagging who is no business of mine! I suppose it's some kind of subterfuge for people who don't have sex lives of their own so they deal with it vicariously through the shenanigans of others. And that's very dismal indeed. It's like you're depriving yourself of your own existence and there's a system called social media that's helping you do that. How insane! But there we go.

HAVE A SENSE OF HUMOUR

I've got this thing that I don't trust people who don't have a sense of humour. And I look at the Republicans here in the States at the moment and it's one bunch of morose, angry fucks. I watched Donald Trump make a speech the other night and the first eight minutes was him just praising himself! At no point did he mention anything about his policies or what the future holds for the rest of us. A politician to me is someone who volunteers to do good for others. It should not be a career.

DON'T ACT YOUR AGE

I really like the people in America. They're very 'outwards', open-minded, fun-loving and adventurous. There's none of this 'act your age' stuff here and I really appreciate that. An example is 85-plus-year-olds bungee jumping out of aeroplanes on a regular basis. Would I do that? 'Do what thou wilt'! Without the rest of the [English writer/magician, Aleister] Crowley sentiments!

ANARCHY DOES NOT RULE

I'm not an anarchist because I think that's just mind games and it's destructive because it offers no viable alternative. Anarchy seems now to be an act of jealousy. I would put anarchy in with the seven deadly sins. I've never appreciated destruction for its own sake. I'm somehow just looking for common sense in life.

HEAVEN IS HERE ON EARTH

I don't make music for personal gratification, I do it just because I'm alive. Owing to childhood illnesses, I'm very grateful. So anything that gets me out and about and expressing my own individuality to me is something that I respect fully. Do I fear death? I don't know what it is, except it is the end. That Bob Marley line [from *Get Up, Stand Up*]: 'If you know what life is worth/You will look for yours on Earth' always meant a lot to me. That's absolutely it. Heaven is here on Earth. Peace.

Ronnie Spector

Singer, The Ronettes

'John Lennon shouted, "Hello, Ronnie Ronette."
He recognised me from the back of my head!'

STICK TO YOUR LOOK

People still recognise me 50 years on from our '60s success because I still look like a Ronette: big hair, eyeliner and lipstick. The Ronettes got it all from the streets of Spanish Harlem in New York in the early '60s. We were half-breeds, mix-raced, so we took our look from the black girls, the Spanish girls, the Chinese girls and put it all together. I remember John Lennon shouting, 'Hello, Ronnie Ronette' to me because he recognised me from the back of my head! I'm still around today because I've kept that look.

KEEP IT SIMPLE

I still have the same routine before a show. As long as I have my lipstick and hairspray I am ready to kick ass! I've seen so much of the divas and it's not rock'n'roll to me. There are so many choreographers and stylists it's a circus.

DON'T HAVE A BUCKETLIST

... Have a fuckit list! Let me give you an example: I ran into Ray Chew, the musical director from *Dancing With The Stars*, and he asked me to be on the show. Initially I thought, 'Jeez, that's a lot of work,' but then I thought, 'Fuck it, I want to win!' I've had hits that lasted more than five decades, so I don't get hung up any more.

RELISH A CHALLENGE

If somebody tells me I can't do something I want to do it more! My mom said it would be difficult to make it as a singer so that made me even more determined. It's a hard business and you need luck. We were signed to Colpix Records and then we met Phil Spector. Maybe if we hadn't met him we wouldn't have been stars. But I was really determined, all I cared about was being onstage.

IT'S NOT ALL PARTY, PARTY, PARTY, DRUG, DRUG, DRUG

If I am not onstage, I prefer being at home, doing yoga or watching TV. If you go out and party, party, party and drug,

drug, drug how can you do a great show for your audience? And it's all about the audience. They pay their hard earned money to see you.

NO MATTER HOW BAD THINGS GET, IT WILL GET BETTER

I've always been an optimist, that's why I'm still living! What makes life better is not thinking about last week, but thinking about next week. So long as I'm singing, that's what matters to me. When I'm onstage I'm not married, I don't have kids, the audience are my everything – I'm making love to them.

BLIGHTY IS ALRIGHTY

The UK has been good to me. When I first came over all the fog and rain made my skin good. I'd go walking in the rain to get the moisture – and London was fun! I remember going to ['60s restaurant] Crazy Elephant with John Lennon or the time we went to George Harrison's house for breakfast after an all-night gig. He had nothing but canned goods! No bacon, no eggs, but we had such fun. Back then there was innocence to music. We had The Rolling Stones opening for us on one tour and we had the greatest times on the bus. Everyone just wanted to make music.

NEVER WATCH YOURSELF ON TV OR READ YOUR PRESS

I did once and never again! I got a great write-up but there was some little thing they said about how I looked and I just went,

'No more!' You think, 'Oh, I look bad' despite what everyone else is saying. The artist always picks out the little things, so don't show me that!

TAKE STRENGTH FROM THE PEOPLE YOU'VE LOST

[Doo-wop singer] Frankie Lymon was my idol and I was devastated when he overdosed [in 1968]. I didn't know about drugs but he made me never want to take them! It was the same when Amy Winehouse died, I couldn't go out for a week, I couldn't believe she was gone. It's surprising the people that keep you going when they pass. Frankie, Amy, John Lennon. If you get negative you're gone, so I'm determined to honour them. After my mother and my sister passed I didn't think I could sing again but I got onstage and that kept me going. I know they're up there looking down on me.

NEVER RETIRE

Rock'n'roll is happiness, it's being in the moment and it's freedom to be who you want to be. I hate to say it, but I don't enjoy anything but rock'n'roll. Not jazz, not folk, not country. I am about rock'n'roll. People ask me when I'm going to retire. Never – rock'n'roll will have to retire me!

Blondie

Debbie Harry and Chris Stein,
singer and guitarist, Blondie.

*'Some of the most popular people in the
world are complete idiots' - Chris Stein*

PLAY THE FOOL

Chris Stein: My favourite thing that I often tell people is something Debbie told me: 'You can never make too big a fool of yourself.' It's something everyone should take to heart, because some of the most popular people in the world are complete idiots.

Debbie Harry: If you can't really laugh at yourself, then you're in really big trouble.

DON'T HITCHHIKE (ESPECIALLY WITH SERIAL KILLERS)

DH: Never hitchhike [before joining Blondie, Harry accepted a lift from notorious serial killer Ted Bundy]. I was recently reading *Carsick: John Waters Hitchhikes Across America* and his adventures were so unbelievable that I walked away wondering if he made the whole thing up. But I would definitely say don't go hitchhiking. Do I look back and think, 'What was I thinking?' No, I knew exactly what I was thinking but I just got lucky.

CS: Well, you got in the fucking car! She got in the fucking car anyway!

TRUST NO ONE

CS: What have I learned from being in Blondie for over 40 years? Trust no one! You need your inner circle like the Godfather had. Never tell anybody outside the family your business.

DO OR DYE

DH: It did get frustrating when people thought I was Blondie. At one point, I did say to everyone in the band that we should all bleach our hair and it shouldn't just be me, but nobody was interested. The only one who ever bleached their hair was Chris.

CS: Yeah, but that was later on when my hair had all turned white anyway so I just wanted to even it out.

GET LAWYERED UP

CS: If I could go back and give one piece of advice to my 19-year-old self it would be: get a lawyer. If you're dealing with something where you have to sign something you need to understand what the fuck it is.

DO WHAT YOU LIKE

CS: Which is what we were doing in Blondie. It was never based on what other people's expectations were, it was just what we were attracted to.

DH: We always started that way. We liked a lot of different styles so we just embraced them all.

ENTHUSIASM ONLY GOES SO FAR

CS: When I'm talking to young people about doing music I always tell them, 'Enthusiasm is not enough.' You have to do your work also. A lot of people are just going on adrenalin, which is part of the equation, but you need to be able to master other things that might be more boring.

DH: Hard work, unfortunately. As they say, 'You have to pay your dues!' I often hear kids who are only just out of school calling themselves 'ideas people'. Yeah, OK, 10 per cent of what you have to do is having an idea, there's another 90 per cent!

AVOID MEMORY LANE

CS: New York is getting pretty cleaned up these days, but nostalgia is a trap too. You have to be able to move forward and embrace what's going on as well.

DH: I've been complaining about nostalgia forever. Who wants to walk down memory lane? We've already done it, why would we want to do it again?

CS: I don't know anybody who wasn't at some point [in the '70s] complaining about how miserable everything was. Everybody was always bitching about how dirty and shitty everything was. But still, it was nice having all the decay.

HAVE INTERESTS OUTSIDE THE DAY JOB

DH: When you have other interests it gives you room for inspiration. Sometimes you get into a lockdown frame of mind and it shortens your vision so having an alternative loosens you up. It could be anything – Chris had a great interest in wrestling at one point.

CS: Was I competing? No, I was just a fan but we used to go to the matches and all that stuff.

GET YOUR ASS KICKED, THEN WIGGLE YOUR WAY THROUGH

DH: I recently read both Ronnie Spector's and Iggy Pop's 10 Commandments in *Q Magazine* and thought, 'Well, gee, I feel the same way!' You get to a certain point in life where you get your ass kicked here, you get your ass kicked there, and you kind of figure it out and you wiggle your way through. That seems to be the way it is – if you're determined to survive, then you will.

Wyclef Jean

Singer, producer

'What makes a perfect gentleman?
Leave big tips, baby!'

KARMA IS GONNA GET YOU

The number one thing I've learned as a musician is: do unto others as you would have them do unto you. I call that the law of karma. You look back and be like, 'I remember when I was 27 this person was an asshole to me.' Or it could be the reverse and be like, 'Oh, this person was great . . .' Now you're in a position to help someone, you're going to help the people that wouldn't have shit on you on your way up.

KNOW WHEN TO MOVE ON

As a producer, when I was working on [1996 Fugees hit] *Killing Me Softly* and the record exploded it was like when I was in high school and they were giving me all this sheet music to learn when I wanted to do my own songs. I liked *Killing Me Softly*, but I wanted to write my own *Killing Me Softly*. On *Ready Or Not* I sampled Enya, but I was like, 'I want to create my own Enya!' With hip-hop you do one record and then you're supposed to do another one and another one, so ours was a unique story. We just knew [second LP] *The Score* was special. Maybe if we had gone on to do two, three, four of them then you wouldn't have got *The Miseducation Of Lauryn Hill* or you wouldn't have got *Gone Till November*.

MUSIC CAN SAVE YOUR LIFE. LITERALLY

When I first started to play music it saved my life. When you're in these communities as a teenager, music gave me a refuge. I was finding myself through poetry, through sounds and that distracted me from being on the block. At times when a shooting was going on, I missed it by 15 minutes because I'd decided to practise this Jimi Hendrix solo.

GENRE IS JUST A WORD

Genre is nothing but a concept. The world revolves around fusion. Carlos Santana taught me that, so I just do music. It could be a song like *Maria Maria* that I wrote years ago – DJ Khaled calls me and he's like, 'Yo, can I sample this song?' So it becomes [Rihanna collaboration] *Wild Thoughts*. As long as it's pure and it's real, it's going to happen.

THINK LONG, LONG-TERM

When I do music, I'll be like, 'In 10,000 years will people still like this song?' People say, 'What's bigger than a hit?' I say, 'A cultural phenomenon.' When you create that, it don't have no colour, it don't have no creed, no nothing. Everyone in every country is just singing it.

GET MOVES LIKE JAGGER

I was doing a gig in Shepherd's Bush in London and I looked up at the balcony and I see Mick Jagger. I told the DJ, 'Stop everything, put one of Mick Jagger's records on so he can understand how he's influenced me.' He was one of those people that made pop culture think about things that it wouldn't have necessarily looked at. For example, he's the reason people in pop culture figured out who Peter Tosh was [in 1978]. People were saying, 'Who's this guy singing with Mick Jagger?' For me, getting the chance to be in the studio with Mick [on his 2001 solo LP] was one of the most mind-boggling experiences.

A PERFECT GENTLEMAN HAS RESPECT

[2000 solo hit] *Perfect Gentleman* was a record I did about how there was a strip club around the corner from school and there was this girl who was stripping and she ended up becoming a doctor. What makes the perfect gentleman? It's that if you go to that bar it's important that you understand that these people have families and they're doing this as a hustle. So the perfect gentleman would leave big tips, baby!

MIX POP AND POLITICS

Before I decided to run for the presidency of Haiti [in 2010] the country was being run by an old regime so I felt like the cycle needed to change. When they took me out of the race I gave my support to [singer-turned-politician] Michel Martelly and it broke the cycle. The idea that a musician couldn't be president went out the window.

MONEY ISN'T EVERYTHING

What's the value of life? Is it billions of dollars? You can have someone who is working a nine to five job, they come home, they're happy as hell. The true essence of life is family and friends.

WORK THE CHOIR

I'm like the choir director. Every Sunday, I see who's working the solo, I do the arrangements to make the congregation feel something. My longevity is based on the fact that I'm composer and conductor. I'm like the hip-hop Amadeus, man.

Ronnie Wood

Guitarist, The Rolling Stones

*'Me and Keith used to see people
drop like flies trying to keep up'*

IF YOU MOVE IN WITH JIMI HENDRIX,
YOU'D BETTER LIKE DOGS

I shared a flat with Hendrix around Notting Hill with
[American soul singer] PP Arnold. That was very interesting.
He went out on tour and said, 'What am I going to do with my
dog?' He had this Basset Hound and asked me to take it. I said,
'Yeah, sure.' So he gave me this dog called Loopy. What was he
like as a flatmate? Very docile. He just laid on the bed with a
guitar. Very stoned, really.

ALWAYS HAVE A NEEDLE AND THREAD TO HAND

In the '60s I couldn't wear a pair of trousers that I hadn't
tapered myself because only I knew how I wanted them.

So I'd get out the needle and thread in the shops and do it myself. We'd always be trying to outdo each other with our clothes. I remember Marc Bolan saying, 'Oh, you got that jacket I wanted!' Me and Rod [Stewart] used to go into certain shops and Marc would be in there and Mr Jagger would be in [Chelsea boutique] Granny Takes A Trip. We'd often meet in the changing rooms. I got it completely wrong once and got an all-white outfit. I ended up looking like an ice-cream salesman!

CHECK YOUR MESSAGES

When I was first getting together with The Faces there was a phone call at the rehearsal space. [Bassist] Ronnie Lane answered it and it was Mick Jagger asking whether I'd be interested in joining the Stones because Brian Jones had just died. Ronnie Lane said, 'Ronnie's quite happy where he is'. I didn't find that out for years, that he'd turned the job down for me.

KNOW YOUR LIMITS

Bobby Womack was such a lovely guy but the writing was on the wall because he abused his body so much. We all did, but I had a cut-off valve and he would surpass that. You'd go, 'Nah, that can't be doing you any good.' A lot of people brought it on themselves. Keith [Richards] and I used to see people drop like flies trying to keep up with the heroin and just being weekend junkies and turning out not being able to handle it.

BE IN THE RIGHT PLACE AT THE RIGHT TIME

I once met Jeff Beck after a gig at the Sheffield Mojo and we got on really well. When he left The Yardbirds I rang him up and he went, 'OK, let's get together.' The Yardbirds got me up onstage once when [singer] Keith Relf was ill. They said, 'Anybody in the audience play harmonica?' My friends pushed me forwards. Afterwards, Eric Clapton sent a message out to the audience – 'Get that bloke back who looks like Cleopatra!' That's how I first met him.

DON'T READ YOUR BANDMATES' AUTOBIOGRAPHIES

When I wrote my autobiography [in 2007] I was very conscious of the sensationalism that I could have done. The publishers want that. They're like, 'Ah yeah! Tell us about being in a bath with Liza Minnelli at this crazy party in LA!' I didn't want the headlines to be the drugs and the hell. The book is forever and if I put something down I can't change it. I said to Keith, 'Have you read my book?' He went, 'To be honest, no. Have you read mine?' I said, 'To be honest, no.' We don't do each other's books.

DON'T LET RONNIE O'SULLIVAN DO A TRICK SHOT OFF YOUR WIFE'S FACE

[Snooker players] Ronnie O'Sullivan and Jimmy White had a grudge match round my place. They were going at it tooth and nail in front of me and Keith. One of their friends had [Rod Stewart's wife] Penny Lancaster stretched out on the table, put a ball on her forehead and said, 'My mate Ronnie can do this trick shot ... ' It went wrong and smacked her in the face. Rod and her immediately left. I never thought the snooker world was so debauched until I met those two.

PUT YOUR FACE ON YOUR ALBUM COVER

We never used to know what our heroes looked like in those days. You'd get a Chuck Berry LP and it'd have a picture of a holly bush on the front – you never knew what the guy looked like. Howlin' Wolf was the same. Jim Reeves is still a mystery. It's only recently I saw some old film of him. He was a good-looking drunkard!

TAKE BO DIDDLEY'S ADVICE

[Wood's first band] The Birds backed Bo Diddley at the 100 Club in London once because his band didn't show up. I said to him, 'Hey, Mr Diddley, our record label Decca, they don't do anything for us. What can I tell them?' He said, 'Tell them to shit or get off the pot!'

KEEP A DIARY

My brothers found my old diary from 1965 in the back of a drawer at my mum's old house. It's jogged so many memories. There's some great things in it like, 'Great night last night, was sick twice.' I kept them from the early '60s to when I first started to get high then I left the diaries behind. There's nothing after 1969. It's all in my head.

Kesha

Singer

*'Figure out what makes you happy
and, quite frankly, fuck what other
people say and think about you'*

DON'T LET THE BASTARDS GET YOU DOWN

I've dealt with my fair share of bastards in my life. Even if they were some total stranger on social media I used to let them ruin my day, or worse, put me in a total emotional downward spiral. I've come to the realisation that you can't control people's opinion of you, you can only control your opinion of yourself. Figure out what makes you happy and, quite frankly, fuck what other people say and think about you.

LET 'EM TALK

'Let 'em talk' is the chorus of the second song on my album, *Rainbow*. It means that when those bastards get to talking about you, don't try to stop them or change their mind, just dance through life and be nice because it's nice to be nice and it's hell to be a bastard. So, be nice or fuck off.

LEARN TO LET GO

Resentment is like the fuel that grows cancer in your body. Everyone goes through hard things and has bastards in their lives but we have to learn to let go of those bad feelings and move forward in positivity.

TAKE BREAKS FROM SOCIAL MEDIA AND GO OUTSIDE

I appreciate social media because it's my way to communicate with my fans, but I have also had to remove it from my personal technical apparatus because it was bumming me out when I was connected too much. Listening to a record or dancing around the house or swimming in the ocean, all of that keeps me present in the world and in life, whereas the internet sometimes feels like it's sucking my will to live.

WWDD? (WHAT WOULD DOLLY DO?)

Whenever I come to a life decision or a fork in the road, I ask myself, 'What would Dolly Parton do?' Dolly Parton is someone I've looked up to since I was a kid. We went to her amusement park in East Tennessee and I knew that my mom wrote a song for her [*Old Flames Can't Hold A Candle To You*] and I loved everything she did or said. She's strong and pretty and independent and funny and works her ass off and does things her own way. Her sayings are words I live by.

IF BOYS CAN DO IT, SO CAN WOMEN, PROBABLY BETTER

Since the beginning of my career I felt like I could talk about boys the way that boys talk about women in their songs. On my new album, a version of that is *Hunt You Down*. I was listening to a lot of outlaw country from male singers. I remember listening to a song where a guy was talking about how he had his revolver in his pocket and he was going to shoot the girl because she was sleeping with his best friend. I was like, 'OK, well, if a man can say that, then I'm gonna write a song about how if you cheat on me, I'm gonna kill you.'

DO THINGS THAT SCARE YOU

I executive produced my last album and made the decision to try to record more like how some of my music idols from the '60s and '70s did with no effects on my voice and most of the sounds from live instrumentation rather than computers. Because I hadn't recorded that way much it terrified me, but now I am more proud of this album than anything else I've ever done and I never would have made it if I hadn't challenged myself.

BRING COLOUR INTO YOUR LIFE

Colour has been symbolic of hope for me. Black will never go out of style and that's just a fact, but personally I was in a dark place a few years ago and the idea of a rainbow full of colours at the end of a storm gave me the hope that I could one day reconnect with that bright, childlike joy again. Everyone has struggles but we can all try to take things that are horrible and turn them into strengths and never lose sight of childhood innocence.

NEVER STOP DREAMING

There has never been a more important time to dream big about who we can be as people individually and as humanity. The world is changing so fast and it's up to all of us to steer it in the right direction. For me, the right direction is towards equality for all, love and protection of everything alive and a rejection of racism, hate, and division of any kind.

LISTEN TO RECORDS ON VINYL

Every album sounds better on a record-player, that's just the truth.

Alice Cooper

Singer

*'I like to wear black when I play golf
because I want to bring a bit of Alice to
the game, but I'm a gracious player'*

BE THE PANTOMIME VILLAIN

Any band, any movie, has to have a protagonist and an antagonist. When I started in rock'n'roll we didn't have a dark lord. Jim Morrison was the closest we had to one, so I created a character with the make-up and shocking jokes. Some people didn't get it. [UK moral crusader] Mary Whitehouse wanted us banned! We sent her flowers every day because we were thinking, 'Thank you. You've helped us sell out Wembley and get to Number 1.'

SNAKES ARE BUILT FOR SUMMER

They get pneumonia easily. We had a couple of snakes get really sick and it makes you feel bad because they're great pets. I give them names, like Boa Derek and Julius Squeezer. When we were doing the House Of Blues in LA, Johnny Rotten showed up. I was holding the snake and it started defecating. They eat rats, so it smelt awful. All the roadies were dressed as clowns and they were throwing up as they cleaned the mess. Johnny Rotten said, 'This is the greatest thing I've ever seen!'

FIND YOUR OFF BUTTON

'Alice' is funny, but only in small doses. For an hour and a half onstage he's intense and fun, but I'd hate to be him all the time. Look at Keith Moon: he didn't have an off button. There were times when I'd say, 'Keith, you don't have to entertain us.' He'd come over to my house for a week and when I got home from the studio, he would be there in a French maid's outfit, cleaning the kitchen. I'd go, 'OK, the asylum is here!' He was a great friend, but he was exhausting.

DON'T BE A BAD LOSER

I like to wear black when I play golf, because I want to bring a bit of Alice to the game, but I'm a gracious loser. If I lose, I look at where I went wrong and figure out how to win. I know some people who wouldn't even give you a two-inch putt. Golf is a game – that's all it is – but it's a game that you can never master and I play six times a week.

KILL YOUR AUDIENCE

If you don't have the desire to take the audience and grab them by the throat, when you're done they'll say, 'Oh, isn't it nice how he did that ballad.' No! Alice doesn't say 'thank you'. If he did, suddenly he's human. Alice is inhuman.

LOSE WEIGHT BY EATING SOMETHING YOU DON'T LIKE

I love a McDonald's cheeseburger once every two weeks, but I know people who eat there every day. If you're having trouble with food, order something you don't like. I had my photograph taken with Colonel Sanders once and I remember thinking: 'If I was a chicken, I'd be more frightened of him than me [in 1969, a rumour circulated that Cooper had eaten a live chicken onstage].' That guy was the Hitler of chickens!

BEWARE THE GOLDEN BUZZ

I was president of the Hollywood Vampires [the LA drinking club featuring Keith Moon, John Lennon and Jim Morrison, among others] and I was on a golden buzz all the time. I was never a falling-down-drunk-type. When they talk about the 'Lost Weekend' [John Lennon's infamous 18-month bender in the mid-'70s], I was the bartender but I got right to the edge. I started throwing up blood one morning, everything was starting to rupture, so I got sober.

SLEEP IS A WASTE OF TIME

I was a distance runner in high school and college and I was on a team that went undefeated. I've kept that runner's body because I'm always moving. I sleep for four hours. I don't want to miss anything. Touring is sometimes easier than my normal life.

BEING COMPETETIVE IS GOOD

In this business, it's important to be competitive. We went from being a garage band to being the best garage band in Arizona. Then we went to LA, the competition was much harder and that made us work. The first time I saw my record at Number 1 and I looked at who was below me, I was embarrassed. I almost wanted to call Led Zeppelin and Paul McCartney and say, 'I'm really sorry.' They were my teachers.

UNDERSTAND THE GREY AREAS IN YOUR LIFE

There was a time when I didn't know where Alice started and I ended. If I walked down the street, I wondered if people would be disappointed if I wasn't wearing a snake around my neck. What killed Jimi Hendrix and Janis Joplin was the fact that they were trying to be their image all the time. When I play Alice there's a personality change. Alice is not going into the audience saying, 'Gosh, I hope you like us.' Alice is whispering, 'Come here.'

Nile Rodgers

Guitarist, Chic

*'I have more computing power in my studio
than the US military had in the Vietnam war'*

DON'T BOTHER WITH SLEEP

I've slept three or four hours a night, sometimes none at all, since I was six. I used to equate sleep with death, so maybe that's still the underlying thing. The amount of times I've gone from nightclubbing directly to the studio … My brain gets active when I start thinking about music, so it's hard to sleep. Therefore, I choose not to.

DEFY DOCTOR'S ORDERS

I was diagnosed with very aggressive cancer. They told me to get my affairs in order. They said that the cancer growth was doubling at an alarming rate. I went out, did a bunch of concerts and wrote a bunch of songs, and one of the first was *Get Lucky* – so I got my affairs in order pretty well!

RELAX, DON'T DO IT

My music teacher told me that the only working definition of discipline is the ability to delay gratification. He said, 'For now, you're gonna play [hums mind-numbing guitar-lesson riff], but one day you'll play [hums complicated practice riff].' And then eventually, I can do, 'Aaaaww, freak out! Le freak, c'est chic!' What he meant was, I'd do this boring stuff so that years later I'd not only get to sing the chorus, I'd write the chorus.

PARTY WITH GOOD PURPOSE

The one time I spent a million dollars on a record was making Duran Duran's [1986 album] *Notorious*. Now, we can't say that it cost us a million just because we were partying ... but [guitarist] Andy and [drummer] Roger Taylor had just quit so I had to keep morale up, and a good way to do that was to party, OK? I remember being at [keyboardist] Nick Rhodes's house partying with Michael Douglas, and Nick's elevator gets stuck. Michael had just done ['80s action flick] *Romancing The Stone*, so now he was Mr Adventure Guy, and he climbs to the top of the elevator and rescues us all. Insane!

TRY TO AVOID GETTING PISSED OFF

It takes a lot to get me pissed off. But yesterday, I'd just landed at Heathrow and the day before my guitar roadie died, when this woman asks me what I'm doing here. I say, 'Charity work.' And she says, 'Do you have any certificate?' I say, 'I have people who work for me that show me everything to do. I'm not being egotistical, I just have no clue about such mundane stuff ...' After 20 minutes of grilling, she still didn't believe me. I had to show her the story on my cellphone, about my roadie's death.

TRUST PEOPLE, NOT INSTITUTIONS

As a teenager, I was homeless. Both my parents were heroin addicts, so I learnt to fend for myself at a young age. But I was lucky that I had a certain way about myself, so I could explain my situation to people, and they'd say, 'Come in, young man, stay over here for the night.' I've been through my whole life without being abused by strangers. Only when I was institutionalised in a place supposed to protect kids, did they abuse me. On the street, people took care of me.

HELP YOUR FELLOW MUSICIANS

I believe in giving back as much help to musicians as possible. Recording with Daft Punk, we were in the same studio we did the first Chic single. They went, 'How did you make Chic records?' So I taught them the technique. We came up with *Get Lucky*, then *Lose Yourself To Dance* and *Give Life Back To Music* in minutes. All three songs were finished in one day.

READ SCI-FI CLASSIC *DUNE*

The latest book I've read was something I first read years ago, [1965 sci-fi novel] *Dune* by Frank Herbert. It's even cooler now than it was then. But as many great things as Frank Herbert imagined, look at what we have in the world now. We have mobile phones and drones. I have more computing power at my studio than they probably had in the US military during the Vietnam war.

DO AS MADONNA SAYS

When I did *Like A Virgin*, I thought *Material Girl* was the best song to lead with. Madonna was convinced it was *Like A Virgin*. But I was like, *Material Girl's* 10 times better.' She taught me that it was about being a girl, losing your virginity, and how relevant a lyric like that would be. Sometimes there's an intellectual component to a record that can trump its primal component.

WATCH MOVIES 24/7

I have movies on every waking minute and I sleep with headphones on because I have to have constant noise. If I didn't, music would be playing in my head – I need something to drown it out. It's a life sentence, man, but the good part is, I get to write *Get Lucky*. The bad part is, I never sleep.

Pete Townshend

Guitarist, The Who

'Morrissey asked me to produce his albums.
I've still got the cards he sent me'

A CLASSIC IS A CLASSIC, END OF STORY

Someone once said to me: 'Aren't you fed up playing Baba O'Riley?' I said: 'The short answer is no.' As a guitar player I have written the song that gives any guitar player the greatest entry moment on any rock song ever. It just doesn't get better than that.

ROBERT PLANT HAS HIS HEAD SCREWED ON

I don't look upon Robert Plant as a contemporary – he's a new boy. But I respect what he's doing. I respect the fact that he's stayed away from Led Zeppelin. I wish I'd had his balls and stayed away from The Who.

YOU HAVE TO KNOW WHEN TO SAY NO

Morrissey asked me to produce albums for him after The Smiths, twice. I've got his notes, his cards. 'Will you produce an album for me? Morrissey.' I did say to [Who manager] Bill Curbishley, 'I really love The Smiths – if I could replace Johnny Marr in the picture there, we might get a really great album.'

TRUST IN ROD STEWART'S TASTE IN WOMEN

I really like Rod Stewart. He was a good guy. He once engineered an almost-relationship for me with the singer in his [mid-'60s] band, The Steampacket, Julie Driscoll. I had a couple of dates with her and I really, really liked her, but I was also seeing my soon-to-be wife. So I had to choose.

IF IN DOUBT, MAKE A CONCEPT ALBUM

I wrote [1969 rock opera] *Tommy* because I thought The Who were fucked. We had descended into comedy singles, Keith Moon was dressing up as Hitler and getting on the front page of the *Daily Mirror*, Roger [Daltrey] had the long hair ... So I decided to write this dangerous piece for a rock band – an extended, kinda pretentious, kinda audacious attempt to change the rock form. I thought it was the only way that we could survive.

THERE'S A WORLD OF MUSIC OUT THERE

I listened to a lot of opera when I was younger. I studied it and I studied orchestral music. I'm not a musicologist but I've got a fairly broad range of tastes – I like jazz, Scottish folk music, Swedish folk music, Romanian, right across the world. I sort of stop at Egypt, unlike Jimmy Page.

OPERATIC TENORS CAN BE ROCK TOO

[Musical theatre star] Alfie Boe did the vocals for the *Classic Quadrophenia* album at my studio in one take. He brings a classical swagger to it, which is a different kind of swagger but it has that same kind of . . . shallow-macho that Roger brought to the original.

WRITE ABOUT A WIDE VARIETY OF ISSUES

The Who went from the unbridled rage of *My Generation* to silly songs like *Pictures Of Lily*, about wanking, and *I'm A Boy*, about whether someone's gay or not, and *Happy Jack*, which is about being bipolar. These were quite issue-based songs, but they were smothered in comedic routines.

MILLIONAIRE ROCK STARS HAVE TO PUSH THE BOAT OUT

I've got seven recording studios but I have about 15 boats. I've only got one very big boat. That's currently in Antigua. She's a big boat, not as big as Eric Clapton's. In the mid-'70s, I used to go to and from the studio in Battersea on the Thames on my little speedboat because I'd lost my driving licence. I'd had a night at Olympic Studios with [Faces' bassist] Ronnie Lane, and my driver had gastroenteritis, so I drove my big Mercedes limousine – never driven it before – back to Twickenham. I thought, 'FUCK THIS GOES FAST!' It was only two miles but the police were waiting for me at the other end.

I DON'T ALWAYS KNOW BEST

When we did the last tour with The Who, I said I would do it if it was [1973 album] *Quadrophenia*. Roger said he would do it on two conditions: I had to give him complete control creatively and complete control of the band. I thought, 'Fuck . . . but I may as well give it a try . . .' It was a bit tough for me, I lost a few players that I really liked and Roger was a little bit of a sergeant major sometimes, but the reviews were spectacular.

Mary J Blige

Singer

'Go to the gym, go for a run, get on the treadmill'

LAUGH

Laugh a lot. Laugh more! Laughing always makes you feel better. It's like medicine, even the doctors tell you to laugh. What makes me laugh? My sister makes me laugh, my friends and a good sitcom. Seinfeld is real funny, watch that! As soon as you turn to it you jump right in [clicks fingers] and you're laughing. I love Kramer, he's just an idiot. He takes it to the next level.

KEEP YOUR WORD

If I say I'm going to do something, I'm going to try really hard to do it. It's hard but you have to try to keep your word because it's important. I've experienced people not keeping their word a lot and it's just so frustrating. So if you say you can do something and you can, make sure you do it. Treat people like you want to be treated.

DON'T BE HARD ON YOURSELF

Don't beat yourself up about things that you can't do anything about. That comes from personal experience. People are always going to use the worst things against you so it's up to you to not use those things against you. Try to be lighter on yourself, laugh about yourself. Don't beat yourself up.

SPEND SOME MONEY

Some, not all. Sometimes you feel like you want to buy something special to make yourself feel good and you should. It's OK to do that. You might as well enjoy your money, because you can't spend it when you're dead ... but make sure you pay your bills too.

SPEAK TO YOUR MOM

Do that as much as you can, if you still can. It's good to talk to your parents and it's not that hard, we've got phones! It's the same the other way too. If you're a parent, spend time with your children. My mum was a singer and she played such good music like Betty Wright and The Staple Singers around the house when I was growing up, which was key to me finding my voice.

FOCUS ON WHAT YOU'RE GOING TO DO ... NOBODY ELSE

If you believe what everybody else says you are, you're going to grind yourself down into the ground. Do you believe you're a good person? Do you believe you're smart? Do you believe you're going to achieve what you need to achieve? Yes! Then don't worry about it. You can't do anything about what other people say about you. You can only affect what you're going to do.

DRINK A LOT OF WATER

It keeps you moist! It keeps your body moving and it keeps you lubricated, it's good for your skin, it's good for everything. Don't over-think it: drink water, it's just good.

WORK OUT

Try to get some cardio. Go to the gym, go for a run, get on the treadmill. It keeps your blood flowing. It's not just about losing weight or being so fit, but it's just being healthy.

IGNORE THE TROLLS

Some social media is just negative. It's people who have nothing to do, so they're going to mess with your life. Are you really going to take some time from your life to say something to them? No! Don't worry about it.

BE POSITIVE

Think positive; be positive. If you hang out with bitter, judgmental people, you become that yourself. If they're saying, 'You're not this' or 'You won't do that', you start going, 'Maybe I'm not' or 'Maybe I won't', I've experienced that! I know it to be true, so don't deal with it. It's difficult to keep these people out of your life – there's so much negativity everywhere – so that's why my earlier commandments are so important: don't be so hard on yourself and their opinion won't matter. Or better still, don't let those people into your life in the first place.

Stevie Nicks

Singer, Fleetwood Mac

'Cocaine almost killed me. It's better to just not do it. Eventually you'll have to stop so start saving your money for rehab now'

MAKE LIKE A BOY OR GIRL SCOUT: BE PREPARED

I'm scared, that's what I am. Before shows, some people – me, Mick [Fleetwood, drummer], we get panic attacks. I have always been terribly nervous before shows. So I am so rehearsed and ready that I could be dead and stand up there and still sing the right words and do the right thing.

THE DRUGS DON'T WORK, THEY JUST MAKE IT WORSE

Touring with Fleetwood Mac in the '70s, cocaine was almost part of the daily routine. But when I talk about it now, I would never want the kids of today to think that I'm saying it was something good. Cos it really wasn't something good. It almost destroyed my life. It almost killed me, and almost killed a lot of people I know. So if anybody thinks it's safe now – it's not. It's better to just not do it. Because you will eventually have to stop, so start saving your money for rehab now. It's so expensive.

LYRICISTS! WATCH YOUR CUSS WORDS

I've been listening to The Weeknd's records. I play them one after the other when I'm in my bathroom getting ready to go out, or just hanging out with myself. He's brilliant. And his voice – he could have come straight out of 1975 – he could have been like Stevie Winwood. He's over-talented. But if I were to meet him, I would probably say: 'You say over and over again words that I would prefer you didn't say. I think they're unnecessary. However, even though I think a lot of your songs are super-dirty, I still really like 'em! So I've given you a pass on that!'

SINGERS! WATCH YOUR SYLLABLES

I saw Adele at the Grammys [Adele had to restart a performance of George Michael's *Fastlove*], and that song was a very hard song to sing for George Michael. It's all about the syllables. I have a song on my *24 Karat Gold* album, *Mabel Normand*, that's exactly the same. That's the reason we're not doing it onstage. Because if you take a breath, you get off the beat. You're one word too late, you can never get back on, and you're dead in the water.

YOU'RE A ROCK STAR - THERE'S
NO SUCH THING AS A SICKIE

Onstage is the one time you can't bemoan how you feel. Even if you have pneumonia, you have to say: 'I'm leaving that in the dressing room and I'm walking out and I'm gonna be great. And when I come offstage, then I can burst into tears.'

WRITING TIMELESS POP OR EPIC FANTASY -
EACH IS AS HARD AS THE OTHER

I love *Game Of Thrones*. [Author] George RR Martin is my age and it blows my mind that he's able to create this vast, interlinked world. As a songwriter I write little movies, but I can't imagine writing even one small book. But then, probably, somebody like him would say, 'I couldn't imagine writing *Landslide*.'

DON'T FEAR THE PRODUCER

In the 24 *Karat Gold* show, I'm singing songs that are new old songs – the ones that should have gone on [Fleetwood Mac's] *Tusk* and *Tango In The Night*, and on [solo albums] *Bella Donna*, *The Wild Heart* and *Rock A Little*. And they didn't: not because they weren't good enough, but because I didn't like how they were done at the time. I didn't like the producers' concept, whether it was Lindsey [Buckingham, Fleetwood Mac bandmate] or Jimmy Iovine. So I pulled them. So the way the songs are recorded on 24 *Karat Gold* is exactly how they were done as demos.

LEARN FROM THE GREATS. AND TAKE FROM THE GREATS

I give Jimi Hendrix, Janis Joplin and [Jefferson Airplane singer] Grace Slick the three nods. From Grace I got her slinky-ness. Janis was just little with a big attitude and big hair and feathers, and a drop-dead amazing voice. And Jimi was completely and utterly humble. So from those three people I got slinky, attitude and humility – and that was my stage performance.

RESPECT OTHER ARTISTS, WHEREVER THEY ARE ON THE BILL

Chrissie Hynde and I have been touring America together. She's just fantastic. A lot of the people in her group say they haven't seen her that happy in 30 years. And I love that so much. Because I never wanted Chrissie to feel like she was opening for me. I wanted her to feel that it was a complete and utter double bill. But because the tour was my idea, I got to go on last, basically.

BE AN EASY WRITER, AND AN EASY ROCKER

I've always loved Tom Petty, from *Refugee* to *Breakdown*, all those songs. Tom's an easy writer – very unlike Lindsey, more like myself. When Tom goes up there onstage, he might as well be in his studio or his living room with the stereo banging.

Johnny Marr

Guitarist, The Smiths

'I spent most of the '90s thinking about the width of my trousers. That's one of the reasons why I didn't form my own band'

CHECK YOUR POST

I was moving house about 10 years ago and I found a cassette that was sent to me [to play guitar on] that I'd never heard before. I put it on and it was an early backing track of three songs off the first Massive Attack album. I just slapped my forehead and went, 'Oh no!!!' To be fair, it just had some illegible scribble on it. I thought it was a demo I'd given to Bernard Sumner that he'd rejected.

START WITH YOUR SHOES

Alec Guinness approached every role by first imagining the shoes the character would wear. He'd then go and find those shoes, in some cases having them made, wearing them and building the character from the shoes up. Who could argue with that? It doesn't end there: the shoes to trouser width and length axis is an important scientific consideration. I spent most of the '90s thinking about that, which is one of the reasons why I didn't form my own band.

IF YOU DO SOMETHING AMAZING, MAKE NOTES

If you're up at 3am and you accidentally create two iconic guitar sounds that you're going to be asked to explain for 30 years, it might be an idea to write down what the hell it is you're doing. I've been asked about *How Soon Is Now?* by guitarists and non-guitarists alike since the day it came out.

LEARN FROM YOUR FRONTMEN

Pay attention when you're around people who are either brilliant, difficult, annoying or all three. My experience of frontmen has been all of the above. Everybody is special in their own way and brings their unique talents to the stage, studio, dressing room and hotel bar. I was lucky to get 30 years of intimate schooling from the best people of my generation before I started making solo records.

IF YOU DON'T KEEP A DIARY, HAVE A GOOD MEMORY

Writing my autobiography has taught me that if you're not someone who keeps journals you need to be extremely present at all times, because you need to make sure that every story doesn't end up with you being the arsehole. Luckily for me I have a good memory.

LAUGH AT YOURSELF

A lifetime of being a Manchester City fan has shown me the value of being able to make fun of yourself. If you now look at Manchester United fans, they're not able to deal with adversity and they're certainly not able to deal with having the piss taken out of them. I do wonder why certain kinds of musicians are City fans and others are United fans. I think it's the difference between being indie and corporate. It's the difference between Mick Hucknall and me.

DO MEET YOUR HEROES

I've been lucky to not only meet my heroes, but to have them become friends. Andrew [Loog] Oldham, Nile Rodgers, David Hockney . . . I ended up being friends with some of them, and they became great examples of how to do it when you get older, too. In the '90s when I was collaborating with lots of people, I would look to Nile and think, 'Well, no one is giving him shit for playing on different people's records . . .'

PUT THINGS IN PERSPECTIVE

Getting close with Chrissie Hynde in 1987 [Marr briefly joined The Pretenders after The Smiths split] happened at a time when I needed it. I was extremely bruised. She said to me, 'Try living with two of your band dropping dead.' I can't tell you what my answer to that was because it would be disrespectful, but it sounded like a good idea at the time, I must admit.

DISCO GETS YOU MOVING

Putting on disco music when I was moving stuff recently was a great idea. You don't want anything that's intellectually distracting. My love of disco started at youth clubs – you could get access to a few hours of great music, wear good clothes and meet girls. I equated being able to dance with being able to get past a couple of players on a football pitch and getting a cross over. Maybe that's why I never made it as a footballer.

CHECK THE CAFFEINE CONTENT

Getting into tea happened because, like always, I dropped other things in a big way. This time it was alcohol and caffeine. But I wrongly assumed that green tea had no caffeine in it. I was drinking exotic tea every morning and bouncing off the walls for 12 hours. I read everything I could about all these exotic teas and narrowed it down to Bai Mudan, which is a magic, golden rock'n'roll elixir that I've brought to every band I've been in since. Doing my own line of tea has been suggested.

Henry Rollins

Singer

*'If it's a choice between buying the record
and missing the meal, buy the record'*

SPENDING TIME AROUND PEOPLE WHO ARE MUCH BETTER AT DOING WHAT YOU'RE TRYING TO DO CAN BE WORTHWHILE

It is good to be with people who are more talented, knowledge-able and experienced in any area of interest or discipline. You can learn a lot, yet still find your own way.

TRAVEL AS FAR AND AS WIDE AS YOU CAN, AND AS OFTEN AS YOU CAN

Mark Twain once said, 'Travel is fatal to prejudice, bigotry, and narrow-mindedness, and many of our people need it sorely on these accounts. Broad, wholesome, charitable views of men and things cannot be acquired by vegetating in one little corner of the Earth all one's lifetime.' I think there is no better way to learn than to get out there and see it for yourself.

THERE IS NO SUCH EXPANSE OF EXISTENCE AS 'SOME DAY' WHERE 'THERE WILL BE TIME'

Putting off anything you want to do for any reason besides the practical is a fantastic waste of time and lowers one's hunger for achievement, risk and adventure.

SOMETIMES ASKING FOR ADVICE IS A SURE SIGN THAT YOU'RE NOT SOLD ON THE IDEA

I often get asked variations of, 'I am in a band, do you think we should risk our jobs and make the music our lives?' I understand that it can be a major decision but I think that if you have to ask, then you have doubts. I never asked. I just went, with absolutely no thought of the future. None.

THE PAST ISN'T ALWAYS SO GREAT

If things seem like they were 'better back then,' you are selling the present and future short. Life allows you myriad opportunities to maximise every second. No matter what awful thing happens in one's life, even in that moment, life is only what you make it.

HUMANS ARE TOO HIGHLY FUNCTIONING FOR SUSTAINED PEACE, SO DON'T WASTE TIME WAITING FOR THE GLOBAL HUG

We shall not overcome. Peace is just a between-conflict breather. You and your family and friends might be cool all the time but the species? Forget about it. We're too survival-oriented. That's why capitalism is such a worldwide hit – it allows one to crush and otherwise devalue one another.

MUSIC IS HUMANKIND'S GREATEST ACHIEVEMENT

I can dig Oppenheimer, Einstein, Hawking and their huge ideas – all of which orbit comfortably, light years outside of my microscopic intellectual universe. However, they can't move me like John Coltrane.

PEOPLE CAN BE EXTREMELY BORING

The internet proves it. Good grief, when was disparaging others anonymously, being crassly voyeuristic and parasitic and so obsessively self-involved such great occupations? Since the beginning of human history. Now you have a far more fertile environment in which to wallow.

MANY OF THE BEST THINGS IN LIFE ARE FREE. SOME OF THEM ARE NOT. DON'T SCREW IT UP

If you have a choice between buying the record and missing the meal – buy the record. When I joined Black Flag I had no money. So I'd sit in Denny's, look at the menu and try and save 35 cents. Then I'd spend those 35 cents on an old blues record. I had to have the record. That was more important. I could eat off someone else's plate later.

VENGENCE IS NOT EXCLUSIVE TO 'THE LORD'

Fuck that. There is not one thing I do that does not involve some quantity of vengeance. I have never had an artistic thought or moment in my life. Every interview, every interaction, that's what I bring. Every gig I have ever done has been a battle. I lost well over half of them but have always swung as hard as I could. I'm still getting back at everybody.

Sean Paul

Singer

*'I don't really do regret.
I think it's a wasted emotion'*

PATIENCE IS KEY

I played water polo and swam for Jamaica at regional competitions. Our coach was hardcore. I spent so much time in the pool I thought I would grow fins, but it definitely gave me discipline and patience for repeating tasks until I got them right.

KEEP AT IT

Never give up ... Ever.

BE THE DADDY

I love being a father. I look forward to waking up and spending time with my son every day. I want to be there every step of the way with him. Becoming a father has refreshed my whole perspective on life. It's all so brand new again.

STAND OUT

My early shows in Kingston were mostly Uptown with a lot of friends there, so they were pretty cool. It was after that, when I had a few songs out there and moved to the next level of shows which were more populated by the general public, when I realised how hard it was to please a Jamaican crowd. It's well known that a Yard crowd is one of the hardest crowds to move. People said I sounded like [Jamaican dancehall deejay] Super Cat, so I guess that made me stand out at first.

NO REGRETS

I don't really do regret. I think it's a wasted emotion. What has happened is gone, it's in the past. We just need to learn from it and move on.

GET CREATIVE

I'm happiest during the creative process. I like writing, being in the studio. I do a lot of creating with my brother, Jigzag. I started producing music a couple of years ago as well. It gave me even more insight into music. I get so deep into that shit now. I just love it.

WORK HARD, BE LUCKY, REPRESENT

Hard work and luck both have something to do with the fact I've been able to carve out a career in music. I think a lot of people don't realise the work ethic that this business demands. It's not just 'make music and do shows', there's promo, video shoots, TV appearances, radio drops, photo shoots ... and interviews. I'm proud of all the awards I've won ... my Grammy, my Mobos, my American Music Award, but I'm most proud of being able to travel the world and carry the flag for Jamaica, and represent for dancehall music.

HAVE A HOME FROM HOME

I've never lived anywhere but Jamaica but I spent a lot of time in Toronto from the age of about 11 to 15. My brother was born there and I have a lot of love for that city and Canada overall. They're always good to me when I go there, whether it's for shows or otherwise.

DISHONESTY IS THE WORST POLICY

Dishonesty is the trait I dislike most in other people. And people who don't have respect for the biz. I've met so many great artists who are so humble, then you meet people who have one or two hits and they act like they are legends and treat others like shit. I hate to see that.

SHOW RESPECT

I've done a lot of collaborations that haven't made it to the public, but I've had some banging ones released. The secret of making a collaboration work is being able to respect each other and give each other the space to do your thing. I'm a student of music and it always amazes me how adaptable dancehall music is to other genres. That helps, too.

Iggy Pop

Singer

'I asked Debbie Harry if I could watch her pee once'

PAINTING IS GOOD FOR THE SOUL

I mean other people's paintings, but also I like to paint. I don't do it very often: 'Well, I'm gonna paint something and make sure I'm still an artist!' I can spend more time looking at art and have better feelings than I do from TV, DVDs and all that crap.

YOU CAN HAVE TOO MANY DRUGS

I once went to a dance music gig in Miami. It's 3am, and this French chick comes up to me, "Allo, Eeggy Pop!" She opens her jacket and she had her drugs arranged in the lining like a tool kit! She had everything – joints, MDMA, powdered drugs, liquid. She was like, 'This is great, I've met Eeggy Pop! At a rave! This is the perfect place!' I didn't hang around. You have to be careful ...

LOOK AFTER YOUR ACCOUNTS

Scott [Asheton, Stooges drummer] was one of those guys – at one point in the band he had lost a quarter-million dollar cheque on the floor of his truck! For six months! That motherfucker! If we got off the road, all I had to do was wait for three months and I'd get a call [croaky whisper]: 'Hey, Jim … it's Scott. Can you lend me 50 Gs?' 'Not 50 Gs again!' After he passed away, I received pictures of his mint-condition Harley, worth, like, 40 grand!

SCARS DO FADE (EVENTUALLY)

I've been around so long that I've gone through these little mini crib-lists of what I'm famous for. There was a period in my life where I'd meet some chick, and she'd say [high-pitched squeal]: 'What do you do? You're not Iggy Pop! If you are, show me your scars!' Then I'd have to show her my chest. Every time they'd be like, 'That's it? Iggy Pop's scars would be bigger!' The night I did it [Pop sliced up his chest onstage at Max's Kansas City in 1973], it looked really wow.

WHAT DAVID BOWIE WANTS, DAVID BOWIE GETS

When he was creating Ziggy Stardust, I wouldn't say David took much of my character, but elements were probably helpful in creating some of the song content: *Moonage Daydream*, *Rock'N'Roll Suicide*. The main thing would be to use the rhyming name.

EMBRACE CHANGE

Working with David Bowie [on 1973 Stooges LP *Raw Power*] was a trauma for the other Stooges because they were hardnuts from Detroit, but I understood that it could be very helpful to us. The music we made before *Raw Power* was very inchoate and sluggish because that's what we were living in, the early heroin disintegration of Detroit. We came to England and, boy, what a breath of fresh air! You'd see Marc Bolan live in Wembley Arena. The Stones were in town. Let It Rock, Malcolm [McLaren's clothes] shop, was right up the street. It was a more literate, exacting environment. David was a benefactor to me, but also to the band. He jolted all of us.

DON'T WATCH YOURSELF ON SCREEN

I've not seen *Velvet Goldmine* [1998 film featuring a thinly veiled Iggy Pop character played by Ewan McGregor]. I did see a clip of Ewan McGregor performing *TV Eye*, which I thought was amusing. But I read the script, and somebody was snorting coke off my ass! Did that happen? Nooooo!

TRY NOT TO BE A LECH

I saw one little bit of [2013 punk club biopic] *CBGB*, where [the Iggy character] horns in on Debbie Harry on the stage. I thought, 'Yeah, that's me!' But no, I've never horned in on her onstage. Offstage? I've tried! Her line would always be [breathy whisper]: 'Maybe when Chris [Stein, then boyfriend] isn't around . . . ' Which was just to get rid of me! I followed her into the bathroom of CBGB once. 'Debbie, can I watch you pee?' 'Maybe when Chris isn't around ...'

GOD CAN HELP YOU ROCK

In 1980 I was drunk at The Ritz club in New York and U2 were onstage. I was on my way backstage to find someone with some blow. As I walked by I heard this guitar riff and I thought: 'Oh fuck! That's the sound of the future.' I read this thing about U2 once that when they started they were like a Bible study group together and really got to know each other. I think that really helped them.

SPEECHES ARE DIFFICULT

I was asked to do the John Peel Lecture. [Comedian] Frankie Boyle had it right when he said, 'Now that David Bowie is giving opinions on the Scottish referendum, I will also respect Iggy Pop's opinions on the CERN Particle Accelerator.' Anyway, I came up with a subject [Free Music In A Capitalist Society], but didn't understand that I'd actually have to write the speech down. Generally, when I write something down it has two lines, repeats over and over at the end, lasts three minutes and we're out of here, right?

Big Narstie

Rapper, MC

*'If you're in a situation where you're a bit
nervous about getting involved, have
a Snickers, yeah? Get some nuts!'*

GET INFORMED

The only thing I learnt at school was how to count. My experience of education was crap at the beginning, but I'm starting to flourish a bit now. What I've learnt is that life is an education in itself, especially learning how to deal with people. Knowledge is power and the person with the most information wins. You know, a well-educated man can take your whole life and everything you own with just a Parker pen and a nice sentence.

DON'T BE LATE

My grandma and mum taught me everything. They weren't rich people, but they were billionaires in manners and respect.

And that's helped me and put me in places where money could never put me. I swear down, manners and respect will take you places that money can't because with money everything's got a time, date and a schedule. Like imagine now if I was late for my interview with you and you've only got 25 minutes, you'd think I was a total and utter prick and you wouldn't like me and the interview would be crap.

CHOOSE YOUR WORDS WISELY

Everyone should be accountable for their words because if you talk shit, you'll get banged. I still kind of live by medieval policies, like the reason why a lot of people didn't get into arguments in medieval times was because if you talked a lot of shit I might challenge you to a duel, yeah? So everyone was really careful about their words and were actually really nice to each other. But nowadays people aren't accountable for their words and actions, so you get a lot of loud talkers who take no action. I'm trying to go back to old-school England with fisticuffs at your local football pitch, you know, like proper English stuff!

WORK HARD AND REAP THE REWARDS

The most important thing I've learnt about life so far is that it is very unfair. But life treats people well if you work hard for it, because obviously you can't choose your beginning but you can choose your end. For example, you were just walking around in your dad's ball bag at a stage in your life and you had no control over whether or not your dad was going to be successful or not, do you get what I mean? It was out of your hands. But now you've made the best out of that and you're a big reporter.

BE A POSITIVE FAMILY ROLE MODEL

It's not always easy but you've got to look at it like this: everyone has to look to someone to take an example from, and it starts from home. The first thing that all human beings learn is by following. So if your mum never says 'thank you' to your dad when you're growing up, then you won't either. So the position you take ... and personally I prefer the doggy style for the creation of life, hahaha, you've got to deal with the responsibilities of it, know what I mean? So you can't be upset about how your child is acting because it's down to you, and understand if you haven't taught your child how to act properly, other people aren't going to spend time doing it for you.

PRIORITISE THE THINGS THAT MATTER

The Grenfell situation still hasn't been sorted out. I think it's really disgusting that there's people living in hotels with mental health issues and kids still haven't got a place to call home. Like before Theresa May had the cheek to say we're going to war with Syria, couldn't she have at least got some nice decent accommodation for her English citizens? Spending thousands on missiles that are going to take lives when you still haven't sorted out lives in England, you prick!?

TREAT PEOPLE FAIRLY

I don't think our bank accounts should determine whether people should say hello to each other or not. I'm talking about fairness and equality between the rich and common man – yeah man, it's right! Everyone's entitled to a bit of common decency, but you can't solve a hundred-year-old problem with a six-month solution. Equality will come, but it takes time. It's all about bridging the gap. I'm quite fortunate because rich motherfuckers like me and I'm one of the poor kids, but I'm not ashamed of where I come from. Wealth gives you freedoms but it doesn't necessarily make you spiritually free mentally.

HEALTH IS WEALTH

Looking after your health is important, but, truth be told, life is weird and unpredictable. In the last couple of years I've known a lot of fitness guys – don't smoke, don't drink, go to the gym four days a week – who've collapsed from heart attacks and died, RIP. I smoke, I drink, I party, I eat the whole shebang, and I'm still here. Thank God.

DON'T TURN A BLIND EYE TO FUCKERY

Meaning, you sitting back and watching something you know is totally not right happen means you've spiralled another reaction in the current events. So, for every person who stood there and watched, the police or bystander or whatever, who sees something that is not right and didn't do anything, you've just made another upset soul who doesn't have any faith in humanity and doesn't believe in righteousness or justice. So how do you think he's going to deal with the next person he approaches? And if you're in a situation where you're a bit nervous about getting involved, have a Snickers, yeah? Get some nuts!

THOU SHALT NOT BE A C**T

It's nice to be nice. Positivity makes the world go round. Every action has a reaction. So if someone isn't being nice and is acting like a c**t, you know how I deal with it? 'Oi!' Slap! 'Stop acting like a c**t.' And Commandment Number 11, the most important rule, man must respect the pum pum, yeah? We all come from womanhood, so respect the pum pum . . . You know what pum pum is, my G? Of course. Haha. Come on.

David Crosby

Singer-songwriter

*'Hard drugs are a waste of time. The time I've
wasted... I could have been making music'*

NEVER TRUST A POLITICIAN

We have a truly horrible president right now. And a Congress
that's as bad as our president. Our government is in the toilet.
They're just the worst that's ever been. Trump is a fool and a
child. I think the institutions of the country and the government are sort of resisting his thrashing around, but he's very
dangerous. I found Obama inspiring. I met him three times – a
respectable, decent, very intelligent guy with a really good sense
of humour.

SET AN EXAMPLE RATHER THAN PREACH

It's a very bad trap for an entertainer to get into. Yeah, it's part
of our job – historically we come from troubadours who carried

the news from town to town – but it's only part. Our main job is to make you boogie, or take you on emotional voyages. People take up the cause of the week, because it's fashionable, or because it makes 'em look good. The ones you wanna admire are the ones who've been in there doing it the whole time and just plugging away at it: human rights and women's rights and civil rights. Trying to make things better. Have I ever been guilty of reaching myself? Sure. I've made every mistake in the book. At one time or another I've made every mistake there was.

DON'T DO HARD DRUGS

Absolutely the goddamn truth. Don't fucking do it. Don't do any of 'em, at all. They're a waste of time. The time I wasted . . . I could've been making music. Cocaine and heroin and speed. That's the stuff. Terrible. If you don't do it, you didn't miss a damn thing. I do know whereof I speak.

TREASURE LOVE

I've learned it better as I've gone along. I've always been tilted that way, but you have to learn how to do it. You have to work at love. It doesn't come for free. I've been together with my wife for 41 years now. Do we still argue? Yeah, sure, but we love each other.

PAY FOR MUSIC

It's a tough thing for us, man. We don't sell records. We lost it. Done. They're taking our music and they're not paying. It's theft. They're stealing it. There's a lot of people trying to figure out a solution. Some new kind of technology might make it right, but in the meantime, it's down to live performance. That's the only way we make any money now. We lost all the money from the records. It's a bad deal.

DON'T BUY ANY OF THE WORLD'S RELIGIONS

I don't think anybody's got the answer and I seriously mistrust anybody who tells me that they do have the answer. Religions have a record of creating problems and screwing it up. That said, I like the current Pope a great deal. He walks the walk, he doesn't just talk.

LET MUSIC BE A LIFTING FORCE

It brings out the best in you. It sure makes you feel good. I write and play every day. There's people that I listen to all the time that make me feel uplifted. Joni, Steely Dan, The Beatles ...

GIVE UP SUGAR

I'm diabetic, but sugar is really bad for everybody. It's not a good food for anybody, let alone diabetics. I eat sugar-free stuff. A sugary treat for me is an apple.

THINK ABOUT HOW YOU JUDGE PEOPLE

I judge people by what have they contributed, what have they created? Who they have helped, what they've made better. Not what they own or how famous they are. I have a lot of heroes in that respect – Pete Seeger, Gandhi, Martin Luther King. Muhammad Ali was a huge hero of mine. People who are courageous. Good human beings.

REMEMBER: WAR IS NOT THE ANSWER

I feel very strongly about it. Not just because I don't like seeing soldiers get killed. A soldier kinda knew what he was getting into. The soldier joins an army and he knows what he's up against. But for every soldier who gets hurt, there are a hundred civilians who never did anything to anybody. Children, for God's sake, getting slaughtered. That is truly evil and what humanity needs to outgrow. My dream for humanity is for us to outgrow war, grow up and go out into the universe and meet whoever's out there. And they are out there, for sure.

Lars Ulrich

Drummer, Metallica

'Metallica is more like a state of mind than a "thing". No one really owns Metallica'

DON'T TELL ANYBODY ELSE HOW TO LIVE

There's a dichotomy here, because my first commandment is: 'Don't tell anybody else how to live.' I'm a fierce believer in individuality, autonomy and everybody exploring their true inner self. As an only child, a loner and someone who felt like he never belonged to anything – even disenfranchised – I've always done my own thing.

BEING THICK-SKINNED ISN'T ALWAYS GOOD

I have this pretty strong ability to compartmentalise. It can be a good thing and a bad thing – it depends. When we lost Cliff [Burton, Metallica bassist who was killed in a tourbus crash in Sweden in 1986] I was 22 years old and I didn't know what was up, down or sideways. At that point, the way to deal with loss was to just forge ahead without even pausing to take stock. I'm really thick-skinned. It's not a good thing, but when you've been called all the things I was called in the wake of [the band's battle with file-sharing site] Napster or other stuff, it's not necessarily bad. I can manage my feelings in a pretty scary way.

BE OPEN TO WHERE LIFE TAKES YOU

I like to consider myself pretty open to the process of ageing. I look at my kids and go, 'What do I have left – 40 years if I'm lucky?' They'll live to see fucking iPhones embedded in your brain or whatever's next. As you get older, there's all this shit evolving in your life. It's very important to be as open to those changes as possible.

ARTISTS: YOUR BAND IS BIGGER THAN YOU

Metallica is more like a state of mind than a 'thing'. Of course, in its most simple form it's a band, but I don't think anyone really owns Metallica. It's something that lives and breathes on its own from all the people who are somehow part of it. Metallica gives me a sense of connecting to something much greater than myself.

PRESSURE – IT'S ALL IN THE MIND

The only time I ever think about pressure is when I'm sitting in an interview and someone asks me, 'When are Metallica going to do this? How will you do this?' I don't relate to pressure outside of the world of interviews.

LEARN TO LISTEN

Exercise patience when people are talking and pay attention. Be sponge-like. I think empathy is not necessarily something you're born with — it's like a craft that has to be honed. The main thing that I learned around [Metallica's acclaimed warts-and-all 2004 documentary] *Some Kind Of Monster*, and the biggest mistake until then, was not checking in with each other more often. At that time, Metallica was this massive machine that sort of avoided how people were feeling. It's very difficult when you've got a machine that size: sometimes the individual can get lost.

MAKE DECISIONS WISELY

Don't make major decisions when you're under the influence of any kind of next-level emotion — if you're pissed off, angry and vindictive or, on the other side, if you're overly elated or joyous.

DRINK ALL OF THE WATER

The first thing I do in the morning is pound a litre of water. As the English say, 'Get it down your neck.' No matter where you are, what the situation, get that fucking water in you. I learned the hard way. Nobody ever told me that growing up in Denmark in the '70s. Drinking water was something you occasionally did if there was no soda.

ROCK'N'ROLL IS NEVER WHAT IT SEEMS

I love the myth of rock'n'roll, but the way that you think it is is rarely the way it is. The biggest myth I can debunk? When somebody says, 'I don't care what anybody thinks', that's a myth. Everybody cares what everybody thinks.

DON'T BE A HATER

Learn the difference between liking something, not liking it, and differentiating between whether it's good or not. Hate is a strong fucking word. You can dislike something, but still find the good in it. You don't hate a Jackson Pollock painting – you just don't like it, or it's not for you.

Ice-T

Rapper

'Your girl might want you to put on some oil and figure skates for her. Just do it. That's jungle sex'

THE REVOLUTION STARTS AT HOME

We're really close to the edge of a civil war in America. It could pop off any time. And if it does, where do you stand? But I'm not preaching it. I'm not gonna get up onstage and say, 'Let's go to war!' A lot of people yell 'Revolution' and they don't have the slightest idea of what to do. Take a little time and clean up your shit before you go running around trying to set something on fire. Shit, what the fuck's the matter with you?

IT'S THE GAME THAT CHANGES, NOT YOU

I've been around so long that all the CEOs of these companies are fucking Ice-T fans. How the fuck do you think I did a Geico lemonade commercial? It's because the people who are making these calls are like, 'I went to college with Ice-T ... Ice-T changed my life ... here he is in this commercial.' Those sort of people used to be scared the shit of me, but the old guard is leaving. That's what I'm saying.

THERE'S REGULAR SEX AND THEN THERE'S 'JUNGLE SEX'

You can be with your wife and you can just roll over on it. That's just sex sex. Jungle sex is when you know what it is that gets you turned on and you build up to it. You're taking foreplay a step further. Your girl might want you to put on some mother-fucking oil and figure skates for her. 'What the fuck?' 'Just put it on and I will fuck the shit out of you.' If you're willing to accommodate the other one's kinks, you're gonna take that sex to another level. So that's jungle sex.

KIDS: RESPECT YOU ELDERS

When my new baby is old enough to understand me, I'll tell her to obey adults no matter who they may be. A lot of people say, 'Only obey your parents.' Fuck that. I believe 99.9 per cent of adults are gonna tell kids the right thing. I don't like kids who say, 'I don't listen to you cos you ain't my momma, you ain't my daddy.' There's nothing worse than a rat-ass kid talking back.

BLACK LIVES MATTER? NO LIVES MATTER

When people came out and said, 'Black Lives Matter', that was a statement of despair. But white people took it over, like,

'We all matter.' No, no, no, no. Can we just have a minute to speak on what we're talking about? But when you get to the true evil powers worldwide, no lives matter. When you deal with the oil companies, with the arms companies who want a perpetual war to go on so they can sell their weapons, we're all collateral damage.

DONALD TRUMP HAS NOTHING TO FEAR FROM ICE-T

Would I ever run for office? Nah. I got out of crime a long time ago.

CONTROVERSY IS OVERRATED

There's a lot of people who think controversy sells records. It doesn't. It hurts you. It causes so much unnecessary shit. With [1992 Body Count track] *Cop Killer*, I found out first hand what it was like to have a whole country after you. The President says your name, you got police all over the world hearing this one guy made this record about killing them. You go in the cross hairs. You're that image that Public Enemy made.

ACTING IS GETTING PAID TO LIE

I learned how to act standing in front of a judge. Acting is make-believe. It's nothing. If you were sitting next to me and I told you, 'The next person who walks in here, convince them you're my manager,' you could do it. Memorising lines? That's easy. I'm a rapper. We train our memories. It's like a strong muscle.

IT'S EASIER TO MAKE MONEY THE MORE MONEY YOU HAVE. BUT IT'S EVEN EASIER TO SPEND IT

If I'd stayed in my single apartment for $600 a month my whole career, I'd have $15 billion in the bank. But you don't. As you start to make money, you spend it. Your lifestyle increases, you have more overheads. Everybody with a job knows that: 'Damn, I'm making more money but I have less money. What the fuck is going on?' Hey, that's just how it works.

ICE-T IS ONE SMOOTH DUDE

I like Phil Collins, I like Sade, I like Enigma. You come in my house, you think you're in a spa. All this ambient music playing. I got aquariums and water features and shit. That's smooth. You're gonna have sex with your girl, you're not gonna put on *Fight The Power*. That's not gonna work. Or maybe it will if you're gonna have jungle sex, I don't know.

Ezra Koenig

Frontman, Vampire Weekend

*'If you walk out of the house in flip-
flops, that's criminally naive'*

ALWAYS CARRY SUNGLASSES

I learned this at Glastonbury. When you're leaving the house
at 7pm, thinking, 'Well, I'm sure I'll be going to sleep before
the sun rises,' you're playing God. You don't know what's going
to happen. When the sun rises, sunglasses are vital to look fly
and protect your ass from the light. Where do I stand on people
wearing them indoors? Withhold judgement. They might be
partially blind, or they've just had their eyebrows done and the
skin's a bit red.

DO YOUR EMAILS WHILE YOU DRINK COFFEE

The best part of my morning is when I'm drinking coffee.
Sometimes, having a coffee is like a one-sixteenth of ecstasy

because you get feelings of empathy for other people. Don't waste your coffee high, use it to do emails because you're presenting the best version of yourself.

DISABLE TEXT PREVIEW

People leave their phones out, they get a text from some crazy person and everyone can see what the text says. I learned that the hard way with an ex-girlfriend. A text came through from somebody I didn't know very well who was trying to make inappropriate plans with me. My girlfriend was saying, 'What the fuck does that say?' You wouldn't want your mail presented to you in a see-through envelope.

RESPECT ALL FAITHS

Growing up in America, I've learned so much from all the different faiths. Linguistically, if you're talking about the Abrahamic religions, there's wisdom in all three of them – words and phrases from The Koran, The New Testament and The Old Testament that can give you an insight on how to live your life. Like the phrase 'inshallah' – God willing: we don't have something like that in English – there's not quite a phrase as powerful.

EAT HEALTHY BY YOURSELF

I think about this in the same way that in a TV show an undercover cop sometimes takes LSD to show he's down with the criminals. You might go out with a person and they want some garbage food, so you gotta go with the flow. When you're by yourself that's when you've got to be low-carb, high-protein. You never know when you'll hit that burger shack with the bikers. You've got to show them you're not a pussy.

NEVER WEAR FLIP-FLOPS IN PUBLIC

Somebody gave me this advice as a teenager in New York City. I was wearing flip-flops and he said, 'You're wearing flip-flops and you're gonna catch the subway?' He explained how a rat could run over my feet. You can wear flip-flops at the beach, at home, but if you walk out of the house in flip-flops, that's criminally naive.

LEARN HOW TO SAY, 'I UNDERSTAND EVERY WORD YOU'RE SAYING, MOTHERFUCKER' IN MULTIPLE LANGUAGES

It's one of the most important things to say if you can tell people are talking about you in a language you don't understand. You hear stories of this happening in cosmopolitan cities: 'Oh, a couple of Serbian guys talking about a girl's tits on the subway because they think she doesn't understand? Well, guess what motherfucker? She's Serbian!' You need that phrase to shut them down.

TAKE A SHOWER

Most people take a shower every day. But whenever you're on the fence and thinking, 'You know what? I took a shower last night ...' take the shower. You're always going to feel better because a shower is not just about cleaning your body, it's about steaming your body. That has a positive effect on your circulatory system and your brain, probably.

IT'S BETTER TO UNDERDRESS THAN OVERDRESS

I mean that in style, I don't want people getting cold. When I was younger I was nervous about going to a party as the only one wearing shorts, sneakers and a T-shirt. Then I flip-flopped. I didn't want to be the only person wearing a tie. It's better to be the guy who looks the most slobby. It expresses a confidence.

DON'T WORRY ABOUT MANNERS TOO MUCH

When you're with children of privilege, there can be a fear your manners aren't up to snuff. But then you realise the fancy people act like bums. They put their elbows on the table and leave crumbs over the place. So don't worry about using the wrong fork. Own it.

Chuck D

Rapper

*'Part of Public Enemy's rage came from
the fact we had nowhere to sleep'*

MAKE A STATEMENT

We came in on the tail of people who really broke hip-hop,
guys like Afrika Bambaataa and Grandmaster Flash who were
singles-orientated, so Public Enemy brought an album stand-
point to the hip-hop game. We did 10 songs on a 12-inch, instead
of two. We pioneered a new level for the art form. The key was
never repeating yourself. We had to make people realise rap
wasn't a fad or temporary or a gimmick. We made statements.
It was hard but enjoyable.

AVOID HOTELS

Public Enemy were full of different personalities – polar
extreme personalities – but all these different characters wound

together to make a statement. What kept us united? Having no fucking hotel rooms. We always slept on the bus. Nothing was easy, but it shouldn't have been. That keeps you focused. Part of the rage onstage came from the fact we had nowhere to sleep.

PROVE THE HYPE

Part of the Public Enemy glory is the story. It's not just a sound. We emerged in a period where that story had to be heard. We couldn't not tell our story. The sonics and the record made the breakthrough but we had to prove the hype. We were representing this new, exciting genre so our challenge in 1987 was to be as intense as any rock band that came before us.

PUT TURNTABLES ON THE NATIONAL CURRICULUM

I was raised as an artist, my schooling was as an artist, my profession has been based on artistry so I can tell you art will set you free, if you really dig it. Unfortunately, most people aren't educated in the arts. One of the best things was after World War II the UK set up all those art schools. Lots of bands jumped to the front because they met there and learnt something. Instruments, turntables, lyrics, art ... it should all be a part of the global education curriculum.

START WITH THE TITLE

I like to write the title of every song down first, on paper, then go from there. The title gives me a direction for what road to take. There's no pressure on coming up with titles. I've never had writer's block, but I have many titles I haven't found songs for yet. The title is the door to your song, so you want it all glossed up so people want to walk in.

BE PAN-GENERATIONAL

One thing I've learnt from being in [supergroup] Prophets Of Rage is that while people are coming to the show as fans of our three bands, we've found from playing live and looking into their faces that there are people in their 20s saying Prophets Of Rage is their band. Sure, they know Rage Against The Machine, Public Enemy and Cypress Hill, but those are their dads' or older brothers' bands. This is a group they call their own.

GET A GOOD FONT

I studied graphics, design and communications at university and when I finished I wanted to give hip-hop graphics a similar mystique to those used by bands like Iron Maiden. I got into the band graphically, before their music. I really loved the Iron Maiden font and I wanted something similar for Public Enemy. What's my favourite font? Impact.

DON'T FEAR THE SUPERGROUP

[Prophets Of Rage guitarist] Tom Morello doesn't like to say 'supergroup', but I think Prophets Of Rage are a super group. We come from superb backgrounds, so when we get onstage the pressure is on to present something that's beyond people's expectations. We have to be super to do that. The other five members of Prophets Of Rage are the best in the world and I have to step up to that every time.

KNOW YOUR HISTORY

I've been a historian from minute one. I felt hip-hop history should be chronicled and preserved. They do the same thing in rock very well, but I feel our art form is improperly curated and improperly preserved. It's a 40-year-old genre and I think we can do a better job of clarifying what it is and what it ain't to the masses, so I'm publishing a book: *This Day In Rap And Hip-Hop History* [out now]. It's important for hip-hop and rap to not just be freestyle. It's important to know the facts and context of what you're doing.

HELP OTHER ARTISTS

I enjoy working with new artists on the SpitSlam record group. I kind of manage it, but we have a philosophy that we don't control our artists' businesses, they choose to let us help them. So, no bank is going to get broken – we don't do loans. Instead, it's like a guild, an association. Servicing artists' dreams and curating their art gives me great joy.

Tom Meighan

Singer, Kasabian

*'Jazz is just background music, it hovers
around the room and offends me'*

GIVE PRAISE TO *E.T.*, THE MOVIE, DAILY

E.T. is like a religion to me. It's always been there ever since
I was a kid; it's my comfort thing, you see. I can remember
watching it when I was three years old and not being able to
understand why *E.T.* wasn't coming back at the end. I'm sick of
crying to it, to be honest. I can be quite emotional. So watch
E.T. every day, my friend. Make sure you've got a nice big TV,
sit back and enjoy the ride.

ONESIES MUST BE OUTLAWED

Simply because 'onesie' is such a stupid word. Is this the way
we're speaking nowadays? Who made that up, man? It's so
student-y as well: 'Let's put on our onesies and lay about all

day and order a pizza'. I saw a Superman onesie and thought I might get it but I said to myself, 'No, Tom. Don't be so silly.' I don't like sandals either and bumbags are sad.

SELFIES ARE SINFUL

I've done them before with my daughter, but I'm not going to do it any more. I just don't see the point. It's all about me, me, me. 'Quick! Look at me on the toilet!' I wish all these celebrities would put their phones away.

AVOID SUSHI LIKE THE PLAGUE

I've tasted sushi but I didn't like it. I remember Liam Gallagher trying to make me eat sushi on his tourbus. Him and Noel were going, 'It's amazing, how dare you!' I wouldn't do it. Maybe I'm missing out. Probably I'm not.

JAZZ MUSIC AIN'T GROOVY

It's just background music, it hovers around the room and it offends me. Loads of people will be very upset by this, but that's how I feel. In my opinion it's people rubbing off at each other, going, 'Ooh, listen to this fantastic music.' Jazz is dead to me.

NEVER CALL A 'TRAVEL DAY' A 'DAY OFF'

A day off is when you wake up in bed and you've got nothing to do. A travel day is when you're at the airport hanging around for a 10-hour flight. Even if it's a little flight, say you're just going to

France, it's not a day off. Our tour manager used to put 'day off' in the diary when it was really a travel day. I think he's stopped doing that now.

COME TOGETHER FOR LEICESTER CITY FC

They're my team. The whole of Leicester's together since we made the top flight. The divisions below that, they're hard to get out of. It can be a long season, man. We've had it shit for 10 years so it's nice to see people happy and buzzing again.

DON'T BOTHER LEARNING TO DRIVE

I never passed my driving test. I shouldn't be allowed to drive. I'd rather be in the passenger seat. Did I really run my dad over [it was reported that Meighan's father had been taken to hospital after the singer accidentally accelerated into him]? That was a freak accident. I was trying to reverse out of a car park because we were boxed in. I put my foot down a bit too heavy and I took him out. He got a nasty knock but he's still here. God was looking on me that day and saying, 'You ain't fucking driving.'

LOVE YOUR FAMILY, EMBRACE FATHERHOOD

A bit of a serious one. Family's the most important thing, isn't it? I'll always be there for them. Fatherhood frightens a lot of people. It certainly frightened me. I remember everyone showing me baby photos years ago and I was thinking, 'Fuck that.' Now I've turned into one of them! So there you go. I was wrong.

STEER YOUR KIDS AWAY FROM ONE DIRECTION

I don't want to take my daughter to one of their concerts but maybe I'm going to have to. Fair play to them. They're ruling the world. I just hope she doesn't fall in love with them. She's only two-and-a-half, so maybe around the age of four she might get into One Direction. I'd rather she was into us but she'd probably call us boring.

Azealia Banks

Rapper and singer

*'Your Queen Elizabeth II rules England.
I rule the world of vagina'*

CRAP JOBS ARE CHARACTER FORMING

I've had some terrible jobs. I once worked as a stripper which
was a desperate trade. Your spirit can easily be broken trying
to arouse drunk men in middle management for a few dollars.
But the worst job I had was selling key rings at the Blue Note
jazz club in New York. There were a lot of handsome older guys
who'd hit on me. I'd be like, 'I'm 18 years old' and they'd give me
a look that was, like, 'That's legal. What's your point?'

ALWAYS CARRY CASH

A woman should always carry at least $75 on her. I've been on
so many dates where you think, 'I wish I wasn't a broke bitch
putting up with bullshit from this guy.' All because I didn't have

the cab fare home. You need emergency exit money. I've had plenty of lean times when I barely had 10 cents to rub together. It's not a nice feeling.

HAVE AN ALTER EGO

One personality is not enough for me. I need to express myself through alternate fictitious mouthpieces. Sometimes I'm Yung Rapunxel, who is vivacious and feisty. Then another day I might be Little Bambi, who is sexy and likes to show her bits but doesn't want to be touched. Finally I have Mariposa, which is the Spanish word for butterfly. My mum worked late when I was a kid and so I was raised by Dominican babysitters and they gave me the name. It means I am flighty and delicate.

BE A 'KUNT'

My fans are called the Kunts because they, like me, control all aspects of their vagina (if they have one) and their femininity. A lot of women grow up fearing their own thoughts and opinions. They don't see there is a lot more freedom there for the taking. Fuck what men think. In my song *Fierce* I say I am the 'C**t Queen' because I am the self-proclaimed figurehead for these women. Your Queen Elizabeth II rules England. I rule the world of vagina.

TASERS AND CCTV ARE GOOD

I think law enforcement in the UK is good. It's far less racial and edgy than in the US. You don't have guns but you have tasers. On the other hand you guys have a lot of CCTV. I've read George Orwell's 1984 and you've definitely got a bit of that going on.

RESPECT YOUR ELDERS

Things are OK with me and my mother now but we used to fight a lot when I was younger. She was born in the '50s and grew up in the Civil Rights era when you had to fight for black rights. It made her angry and that caused me problems. I am from a more entitled generation. But I have learnt to respect her struggles.

KEEP NICK GRIMSHAW BUT GET RID OF NANDO'S

Having Nick Grimshaw invite me onto his Radio 1 show was such a big deal for me. It got me known and I started getting paid properly for the first time in my life. I love the UK for that. On the other hand, I cannot believe that you guys don't have better chicken than Nando's. The spicing is not good. Someone needs to open a Dominican chicken joint there. It'd blow Nando's out of the water.

KEEP 'KANYE' UNDER CONTROL

Kanye is the name of my guinea pig. He's got a bit of an attitude and my two cats are always trying to take him out. He antagonises them through the bars of the cage. One day he'll be lunch unless he realises that his position in the food chain is much lower than a cat's.

FOLLOW YOUR HEART

I was at a New York performing arts high school called LaGuardia. Robert De Niro went there as did Al Pacino, Liza Minnelli, Suzanne Vega and Jennifer Aniston. It's daunting to be at such a prestigious place with all that history. But I walked out when I decided that music was for me and not acting. It's a big life decision but you have to follow your heart.

TWITTER IS FREE THERAPY

People have said I'm a bigot because I've had a few battles on social media. But really I am not. It's just that places like Twitter are like a walk-in therapy suite. You forget yourself. I've said things which in real life might have earned me a slap round the face. But actually I am thoughtful and considerate. So, don't let social media turn you into a monster.

George Clinton

Frontman, Parliament/Funkadelic

*'I've still got energy because in the past I didn't
do much other than sit around getting high'*

FUCK IT

The best advice I give to people is: 'Do the best you can ... then fuck it.' You can't beat yourself up wishing you had done it differently. If you've done the best you can, forget it!

DON'T HAVE ANY REGRETS

If I could go back I'd be reluctant to tell myself not to do certain things. I could say, 'Don't do drugs or don't do this' but even the stuff that's messed me up I've had to come through it and straighten myself out. I've had a good and enjoyable life. I've still got energy and I think half of my energy is because in the past I didn't do much other than sit around getting high! I feel better now than I've ever felt in my life.

IT'S HIP TO BE SILLY

When we started out we had suits but as we had our first hit record in '67 [with early band The Parliaments], here come The Rolling Stones and The Beatles wearing old jeans with patches on and that became hip, so we had to jump ship and catch up quick. We went crazy. We went anywhere we could to find silly shit to put on. I wore a sheet, I wore diapers, I wore tutus ... We wanted to be as absurd as possible.

KNOW WHEN TO CUT YOUR HAIR

Having my long hair and braids was cool when I was younger but once I got older the braids would fall out here and there, I was worried about people snatching them out. If I'd have been running around New Jersey in the last five years with all that I would have been laughed out of town, so I cut it.

SPACE IS THE PLACE, THE SEA AIN'T

The Who's *Tommy* gave me the idea for a funk opera. I thought, 'Why don't I put black people in outer space?' You hadn't seen any, apart for Uhura on *Star Trek*. So we made the record *Mothership Connection* and I told the label, 'Get me a spaceship.' It cost half a million dollars. When we decided to go underwater, that was a catastrophe. Our tour manager had these two 500 pound dolphins made of cement that he wanted to fly over the audience. I said, 'Hell no!' We played in Madison Square Garden one night and the tanks of water we were meant to play behind turned up in Milwaukee!

DO YOUR HOMEWORK

When I made [1976 album] *The Clones Of Dr Funkenstein* I was picking up on shit like DNA and cloning before anybody knew anything about it. People didn't know nothing about DNA until the OJ trial! Before I made the album I found a book on cloning on a train in Dallas airport, as soon as I got off the plane I went straight to the library to find out about cloning.

LISTEN TO THE KIDS

The kids are the key to it all. Soon as you start feeling threatened by the next artist that's coming up, that's the one you need to pay attention to. When I got the call to work with Kendrick Lamar my grandkids were going, 'This is the one, you should do it.' Me and Dr Dre were really close. Every star he produced I made a record with – Tupac, Snoop . . . You learn from them if you pay attention.

MAKE TIME FOR A LINE

Whenever I get to a place that's got good fishing I get me a line. It's important because I don't slow down for most of the time. Fishing is one of those things that lets me chill and I can think of songs while I'm fishing because you don't catch fish very often!

EVEN PRINCE DIDN'T KNOW
HOW GOOD PRINCE WAS

I was in awe of Prince's guitar playing. With his songwriting and his keyboards he had a new thing going on and he knew it, but I don't think he realised how good his guitar playing was until he did that thing for George Harrison, *While My Guitar Gently Weeps* [playing with Tom Petty for the 2004 all-star live tribute]. He told me when Eric Clapton told him to play that solo, then he knew something must be up!

THE FUNK CROSSES GENERATIONS

People tell me they're bonding with their children because they all like Funkadelic and different periods of the group. I've always had that with people in jail. People that have been in there for a long time knew *Maggot Brain*, people that went in when *Give Up The Funk* was a hit knew the *Mothership*, then you got the whole world of Snoop, Dre and everybody else who knows the funk through the samples.

Father John Misty

Singer-songwriter

*'My beard smells like juniper and rose water
and the unguent that I drip of personal charm'*

ALWAYS LISTEN TO YOUR PUBLICIST

Your publicist knows what's best for you and your career. Talking to fancy magazines may seem like a waste of your time but there's a reason you get paid to sing and they get paid to think for you.

CULTIVATE 10 RULES BY WHICH TO LIVE

Eight is lazy and morally reckless, and more than 10, and you run the risk of running a joyless, legalistic life devoid of spontaneity.

ALWAYS BE PUNCTUAL FOR INTERVIEWS

The interviewer has to spend all day listening to guitar players pedantically explaining the effects of global warming, the true nature of spirituality and the dangers of social media. So try to be respectful of what precious little time they have left over for heavy drinking and staring into the middle distance and asking themselves why they ever started listening to music in the first place.

DON'T BE SARCASTIC OR META

These are short cuts to cleverness. Speak from the heart and humbly accept that people might actually want to know what you think, hard as that may be to believe as you attempt to watch season two of [turn-of-the-century medical drama] *The Knick* while giving an interview.

ALWAYS REMEMBER TO PROMOTE YOUR ALBUM

With so much to say about such a broad range of topics it can be easy to forget that the most fundamental reason we're here, you and I talking, is a craven, cynical attempt to trick people into buying my album based on glossy, airbrushed pictures of my well-oiled beard which smells like juniper and rose water and the unguent that I drip of personal charm.

DON'T DO TOO MUCH PRESS

At some point you will become fatigued and, more dangerously, lose perspective. You will appear in fashion spreads wearing $4000 suits covered in the spittle of white tiger meat kebabs as you have disparaged graphic designers with your mouth full. You will, when asked simply how you are doing, explain to friends and family what the thought process was behind your newest release at Thanksgiving dinner.

DON'T MENTION FAMOUS PEOPLE

No matter how lulled by a sense of fraternity the interviewer's narcotically lilting accent has you, don't reveal the story about how it was actually you who broke Florence Welch's foot or that all the songs on Adele's 21 are about you.

LEARN TO IDENTIFY THE WARNING SIGNS OF A POTENTIAL PULL QUOTE

Typically, the pull quote-baiting questions come right at the end of an interview when trust has been established and your guard is down. The interviewer will say something like, 'Well, that should be good for me, oh, one last thing …' Which is for some reason a dog whistle for opinionated people who have spent the previous 45 minutes meticulously disfiguring every thought they have into a bland universal platitude that it is time to take direct aim at Noel Gallagher or graphic designers.

DON'T READ YOUR OWN PRESS

They can never portray you as brilliant and honest and funny as you know you are.

DON'T START BEEF WITH NOEL GALLAGHER

You won't win, that guy is going to live forever and he never forgets.

John Cale

Singer/musician, The Velvet Underground

*'I thought it was such a big mistake to fire
me from The Velvet Underground'*

COMMUNICATION IS ESSENTIAL
FOR YOUR SOUL

Improvising music has been a real lifesaver for me. From not
learning English until I was seven [Cale grew up speaking
Welsh], to going to America … improvising was the way I
communicated. You may not be able to order a cup of tea
with music, but you'll make a friend, and then maybe they'll
offer you one.

FIGURE OUT WHO'S RUNNING THE SHOW

I worked as an exec at a label [Warners] for three years in the
'70s. I really learnt how corporations work and why you need to
figure out who's in charge, because that's the guy you're going to

eventually answer to. Then one day I decided it wasn't for me. It was comfortable getting a pay cheque, but I really wanted to be onstage.

FIND THE RIGHT VEHICLE

You have to pair up with the right people. I produced Happy Mondays' first LP because of [Factory records boss] Tony Wilson. He was probably the most dangerous man in England. He read the local news on TV and had his own record label – so subversive! I didn't know who the Mondays were, but I said, 'Yeah' because he asked. They were fun!

STICK TO YOUR PRINCIPLES

Those early Velvet Underground shows were down to pure determination. Imagine: viola, bass, guitar and two voices going in three guitar-amplifiers and what kind of noise that was! It was horrendous, but you keep going. Just follow your principles and eventually it works.

MISTAKES ARE USEFUL

You have to let artists do as much as they can because you want as much of them on the vinyl as possible. That's what I did when I produced Patti Smith [1975 debut *Horses*] and Iggy Pop [The Stooges' self-titled 1969 debut]. You want their personality, their foibles, their mistakes, in there. I found mistakes could be really useful as a producer because it put you on a journey together.

SILENCE SHOULD SET ALARM BELLS RINGING

When I was fired from The Velvet Underground I thought: 'Well, I should have seen that coming!' We'd been doing shows where we didn't talk to each other and in the studio we had a room each. We were four people who couldn't be around each other any more. I thought it was such a big mistake to fire me but between the touring, the drugs, the management and all the other activities, ultimately Lou didn't want to keep the band together. So be it.

WORK IS MUCH MORE FUN THAN FUN

When I left The Velvet Underground it made me very determined to do my own thing. I went off and produced [1968's] *The Marble Index* for Nico and then Iggy. I was really determined to make it work because ultimately work is more fun than fun.

IGNORE THE RULES

Whatever you're doing, try it differently – put a right-handed cup in your left hand, whatever. If you've got a song and the guitar is playing a particular line, give it to another instrument. Throw the rules out the window.

REVISIT YOUR PAST BUT DON'T REPEAT IT

I love going back to old songs but changing them around. Yes, I could do them really well but it's much more interesting figuring something else out – 'Instead of Nico, let's get a choir!' I learn so much about the material, particularly when you do it with different musicians. It's a good source for ideas.

STOP TRYING TO MAKE A KILLING AND MAKE A LIVING

When I was at the label I thought I knew about songs and I knew campaigns so I thought I'd write the song about this, hook up with that, and it would all work out. Then one of the promotion guys gave me this advice, 'Stop trying to make a killing and make a living' and it made sense. Take care of the basics, you can't always depend on grand idea.

Charli XCX

Singer

*'Onstage I make weird faces, sweat
a lot and show my pants'*

DANCE AT ALL PARTIES

This is a life rule I only began to appreciate after an awards ceremony the other month. I got to the party and danced for three hours straight. It was amazing! It was like a free drug. It puts you in such a good mood. The other good thing about dancing is, generally, you don't have to talk to other people, which is another bonus. What if no one else is dancing? You start it! It's a risk, but one worth taking.

USE EMOJIS WISELY

There's nothing that annoys me more than when people don't think their emojis through. If you go down the emoji road you need to have a 'top three favourites' that sums up your personality. Mine are the painted nails, a pizza slice and the pink heart with the two yellow stars, which basically means I'm sassy, hungry and cute. My mum is always sending me millions, it doesn't help me understand the emotion she's feeling, it just makes me think she's having a panic attack. What does a ghost next to a surfer actually mean?

NEVER FORGET YOUR MUM'S BIRTHDAY

That's a crucial one. I've done it before and she was not very happy at all. It's not that she'll be angry at you, she's your mum; she'll just think you're a moron, which is worse. When is my mum's birthday? Er, it's around 20 October . . . she's going to be so mad when she reads this!

WRITE A DIARY

I did this a lot when I was younger but I always wrote diaries as if someone was going to read them. I've started doing it again now but writing about what's happening. Everyone in their life does so much so it's nice to have the hard evidence of being a human being. Have I re-read the early ones? Oh my God, yes! I found one that was about going to my school disco, it was so embarrassing: 'In a couple of hours' time I'll be at the school disco grinding up on some hot boy. Will it be Rory? Will it be Macca? I don't know, but I can't wait!' Cringe!

DEFINITELY MIX CHAMPAGNE AND VODKA

I drink vodka, champagne, orange and cranberry juice plus a squeeze of lime all together. It shouldn't work but it does. It will give you a hangover, but it's a nice dreamy hangover and they're always really good because you can eat pizza in bed.

ALWAYS CARRY RED LIPSTICK

This only really works for girls, drag queens and David Bowie. It's a classic lifesaver. It's so chic and it makes everything feel that tiny bit better. Also red lipstick is genius because it hides red wine lips really well.

ALWAYS CARRY SPARE HEADPHONES

I'm always losing them and whenever I'm on a plane and not got some I'm sat next to someone who really wants to talk for the whole journey. It's a life necessity!

FREAK PEOPLE OUT

I generally do this onstage. I make weird faces, sweat a lot and show my pants. If everyone let go they'd feel more alive. When I supported Katy Perry there was an area in the crowd for VIPs who are so close to the stage they can see up your skirt. It's so funny because you can see it really gets the kids' dads! They get on edge: 'Oh my God, what's happening?!'

STAY IN TOUCH WITH YOUR YOUNGER SELF

When I was younger I had a lot of hopes and ideas – I still do, I'm not totally depressed yet – and many of those were exciting because I didn't really understand the parameters or the rules. I wrote [Icona Pop's hit single] *I Love It* when I was 17! Have I thought perhaps I shouldn't have given it away? No, I don't regret giving away any songs. Not yet …

HAVE A CURVEBALL AMBITION

Even if you're set up for life, always have a total left-turn dream just in case. For me that's becoming a professional ice skater. I'm nowhere near close but I think it would be really cool. I've been ice-skating in a miniskirt – you know, bare knees – so that's pretty confident. I went with [former Disney star] Nick Jonas! The whole thing was really weird. It wasn't a date or anything, but the day I released my album I went ice-skating with Nick Jonas in a miniskirt. That put the idea in my head …

James Blunt

Singer-songwriter

*'Say what you like about Take That, but Mark Owen
got more action than Noel and Liam combined'*

YOU ONLY NEED ONE SONG

Some people take years and multiple albums to make their mark.
Fuck it. Live fast, let your career die young. Take The Rolling
Stones, for example. After all these years, they're still trying to
achieve what *You're Beautiful* did in just four weeks. They must
be pissed off. I tried to introduce myself to Mick once, and he
was having none of it. I totally understand. I'm feet up by the
pool while he's still slogging it out trying for the big one.

THERE IS NO SECOND COMING

This counts for so many things. Sexually. My career. But mainly
what I'm getting at is that no one is coming to save us, so we
need to fix things ourselves now.

IT WON'T SUCK ITSELF

And the likelihood is that no one's going to do it for you either, so you're going to have to do it yourself. And you know what? If you want things done properly, you have to do it yourself anyway. You reach for the stars if it's worth it – so keep trying.

UNDERSTAND PERSPECTIVE

I've started playing the ukulele and make my band stand at the back of the stage so that I look bigger. It totally works. Most people who stop me in the street say, 'Hey, you look just like James Blunt, only smaller.' Things aren't always as they seem.

LIFE IS NOT A DRESS REHEARSAL

And it's short too, so don't waste your life wishing for a better one. There would be nothing worse than reaching old age saying you wanted to do something, but never had the courage to do it. Is there anything I regret not doing? Well, no, surely there's still time?

OPINIONS ARE LIKE ARSEHOLES (EVERYBODY HAS ONE)

It's really tempting to think my opinion is fact, but it's not – it's just my self-serving opinion, and really, I should keep it to myself. Just because they invented Twitter, it doesn't mean my opinion is in any way validated.

FOCUS ON THE POSITIVES

We focus on the negatives so often. Say I played in front of 20,000 people and instead of focusing on the people who came to the concert we focus on the one negative tweet when the person who wrote that one negative tweet is probably on his own at home with his trousers round his ankles playing with himself.

TAKE THAT GOT LAID MORE THAN OASIS, SO JOIN A BOY BAND

No, really. They did. I know you don't want to admit it, but look at the stats. An audience of beer-swilling lads arm in arm football-chanting *Wonderwall*, or an audience of screaming girls chasing you to your hotel, and breaking in through the fire escapes to get to you. Say what you like, but Mark Owen got more action than Noel and Liam combined. And he doesn't get drunk blokes coming up to him in the pub trying to be his mate. No wonder the Gallaghers are so miserable.

CREATE LUCK

People aren't lucky – people create luck, so take risks. Basically, I'm saying it's a numbers game. Be everywhere, and eventually, you'll be in the right place at the right time. You get lucky by creating opportunity.

MIDDLE OF THE ROAD IS MORE DANGEROUS THAN ANY OTHER KIND OF MUSIC, SO FUCK OFF WITH YOUR WHINING

It's all well and good you shouting from the safety of a pavement about how uncool MOR music is, but then you can – you're on the pavement. We're the dudes who are living dangerously in the middle of the road, with oncoming traffic and no central reservation. I'm like Nigel Mansell. You may think it's dull as fuck, but that's just because we make it look easy (listening).

Tricky

Rapper

*'Beyoncé started sexy dancing into me
onstage at Glastonbury. I'm a shy lad, really.
I liked it but I wasn't pushing back'*

VILLAINS ONLY UNDERSTAND VIOLENCE

This is a country of villains. Some of them look like villains. But the ones who don't are the ones to look out for. I got mugged by an old manager and I lost a lot of money. But the thing is the respectable villains talk nicely and smile. They don't go to jail. They use the law to get away with things. I am not a street guy who takes revenge with my fists or a car tool. Sometimes I wish I was. Villains only understand a kicking.

DON'T CALL YOUR HOUSE A HOME

Home is not a building. It's a feeling you have as a child before the onset of responsibilities. When I think of being a kid in

Knowle West [in Bristol] being looked after by my gran, that is home to me. Running free. Taking liberties. Since I've enjoyed success I've lived in LA, New York and Paris. I moved back to London last week. None of them places gives me a feeling of home. But you can't go back, man. You can't.

YOU NEED BALLS TO STAY IN A POSH HOTEL

Because of my face sometimes people think I can't pay for things. I was in this health food shop the other day. The girl said, 'Can I help you?' in a way that means she thinks you are robbing. When I offered to give her my wallet while I browsed she went too far the other way. She was like, 'We have raisins on special offer, sir'. I feel embarrassed in posh hotels too. I stayed in the same one as 50 Cent once – even he's more confident than me. And he is a villain! He's been shot! He acted like he owned the place.

DON'T DISAPPEAR UP YOUR BUM

People ask me when I'm going to do more music with Massive Attack and we did three tracks at the end of last year. But there is an ego problem there. For example, Daddy G walked past a cousin of mine he's known since he was a baby. That's disrespectful. Massive Attack has become this thing. But one day they won't have it and then what do you do? When I meet fans I don't want to be Tricky. I say, 'Let's have a drink but just as people.' You have to hold on to the person you are.

WOMEN ARE TOUGHER THAN MEN

My mum died. My dad wasn't around. All the men around me were fighters. But women are tougher. I don't know any men who'd lay down their life for a child. When I was in a relationship with Björk I didn't realise she was like that. She would've been good for me but I couldn't see it ... The track *Valentine* on my new LP [*False Idols*] is my thank you to her. She's a great person.

DON'T FORGET YOU'RE AN ADDICT

I smoke a lot of weed. A lot. Sometimes I stop, feel much better and get more done. But then I forget I've given up and start again. I'm an addict, no two ways about it. Smoking weed has got me in some weird situations. I was in Jamaica once with Chris Blackwell [founder of Island Records]. We were in this dark hut and there was a coffin in front of us. I said, 'What's that?' He said, 'It's a Peter Tosh tribute coffin for keeping gear in'. He said he could get me one. That was too weird. I said, 'I don't need a fucking Peter Tosh coffin, I need to go to bed!'

DON'T EXPRESS YOUR FEELINGS IN THE NICK

I found the nick hard cos I need women around me [Tricky served six months aged 17 for buying forged £50 notes]. I have friends and family who can do time like it's a fortnight in Benidorm. You have to be made a certain way for that. I know this is going to sound a bit weird ... I'm not gay but I saw a beautiful boy today. He was in London carrying his guitar. He looked cool and beautiful. I'm not gay but you can't express those feelings in a nick. You'd get beaten up. Or worse.

BEWARE OF DAVID BOWIE

He's nice but weird. When he wrote all that stuff about me [Bowie wrote a surreal eulogy to Tricky in Q in 1995] it blew my mind. Partly cos it was great writing. I quite fancy myself as a shaman. [Bowie called Tricky 'a shaman that had never slept with The Others'.] Especially after a smoke. I'd never even met the guy when he wrote that. Then he came to see me after a show and had a photographer with him. That freaked me out. Anyway, when I rang him afterwards to say we should work together his people said he was busy.

ALWAYS TAKE CARE OF BUSINESS

I think people who understand how the law works are geniuses. I used to have this house in New Jersey. And then one day a lawyer told me that I didn't have it anymore. It got taken away from me. How the fuck did I lose a house? I have no business idea. I missed the lesson on taking care of business.

HUSBANDS SHOULDN'T WATCH
THEIR WIVES PUTTING OUT

Doing Glastonbury with Beyoncé was beautiful madness [Tricky guested during Beyoncé's headline slot in 2011.] She's a nice-looking girl but I don't really know her music. But of course I said yes. When my mic stopped working, for me it was,

'What the fuck?' But she went into another professional gear. She came over and started sexy dancing into me. I'm a shy lad really. I liked it but I wasn't pushing back. Jay-Z was watching us, which was weird. No husband wants to watch their bird putting out to another geezer at Glastonbury do they? Unless he's mental!

Brian Wilson

Singer, The Beach Boys

'Would I recommend LSD? No'

ALWAYS TRY TO BELIEVE IN YOURSELF

This is very crucial – paramount if you want to enter into the music business. I didn't believe in my talent too much until I was about 20 years old, then I thought I was pretty good. And make sure you master your instrument before you first start recording. Is it advisable to work with your brothers? Yes, it's a good idea to keep it in the family.

KNOW YOUR PHARMACEUTICALS

Don't take the wrong drugs is my advice. Medicine is OK, but not drugs. Do I trust doctors? Yes, very much. Would I recommend trying LSD? No. I would say don't ... don't ... [starts singing]. OK.

YOUR BODY IS A TEMPLE.
TREAT IT WITH RESPECT

I say do a little exercise every day and eat vegetables. I run, I eat vegetables ... well, I stopped eating vegetables but I'm going to start eating them again. I take a lot of vitamins.

DON'T SMOKE. THOSE THINGS WILL KILL YOU

I quit 12 years ago. My wife said, 'Look, it's time to get off the cigarettes, you'll get lung cancer'. I said, 'OK', so we put me on the patch. I put a patch on, patch 21 [milligrams of nicotine], then patch 14, patch 7. Three times, all done. No trouble.

TAKE CREDIT WHERE CREDIT'S DUE

It embarrasses me to be called a genius, but I accept it graciously. It makes me feel fine.

YOU CAN'T MAKE IT WITHOUT THE
LOVE OF A GOOD WOMAN

I've learned that women can be hot for you. They can also be friends. Dating? I always used to take my wife to movies. So you've got something to talk about afterwards? Yes. My wife keeps me grounded. I couldn't do it alone.

FACE UP TO YOUR FEARS

I face them with courage. When I get ganged up against by people I have a lot of courage. Is that something that still happens now? Yeah. In business dealings? Right, yes, exactly. I respect courage and personality and ... that's it. Courage and personality.

TREAT PEOPLE NICELY, EVEN IF YOU'RE AFRAID

My worst vice is being nervous. I'm scared all the time, usually. How do I cope with meeting new people? I just do. In conversation you can pick up whether someone is a cool person, now and then that'll happen but I don't know until after I get to know them that I can really trust them. Friends are very important to me, so I'm open. I treat people nicely, very nicely, and I would like to be treated coolly.

CASH ISN'T THE BE-ALL AND END-ALL

Money makes me a little happy but not really happy. Doing a good concert for people makes me happy. What financial advice would I give? Keep enough in the bank.

IF YOU WANT TO CUT A DASH, WEAR BLACK

It's a very, very, very ethereal look.

Josh Homme

Frontman, Queens Of The Stone Age

'Everyone says it's a small world. It's not.
Have you ever tried to walk it?'

NO ONE KNOWS

Everyone's always trying to tell you, 'You know what the truth is ...' and then their face makes noise and they know everything. But I don't know anything. I know that. That's the one thing I know really well. I know jack shit.

QUESTION EVERYTHING

I look at rock'n'roll as a positive force, as a great inspirer of questioning everything and being a realist and saying, 'This is all a bit fucked, you know that right, but we do *this thing* that creates idealism and optimism.' That escapism allows you to trip and fall on your thoughts and when you trip and fall on your thoughts, there they are on the floor under the couch.

ENJOY YOURSELF

The greatest thing I took from working with Iggy Pop was 'enjoy yourself'. Because you can't expect anyone else to enjoy yourself. It should emanate from you as some sort of contagion, magic elixir that's contagious.

DEFY CONVENTION

I love it when someone says, 'You're supposed to do this.' I love to be like, 'OK, so we're *supposed* to do this, huh?' I love poking fun at convention because it's funny. Stop lights are amazing, right? They regulate traffic, they stop accidents, they keep the flow going. But at three in the morning, if you look and there's no one coming and it's the colour red, should you stay there? I think you should only stay there if there's a police officer there and if there isn't a police officer there, you should go. I appreciate the colour red as much as the next guy, fuck, my hair's red, but do we really have to listen to colours at three in the morning?

DON'T WASTE YOUR NOW

You may have thoughts of tomorrow and beautiful memories or regrets of yesterday but they don't amount to much when we're here now. This is all you'll ever get. Even if you have a little anger, it needs to transition into 'hallelujah' as quick as possible so that you can make that now worth it, so that you don't waste your now on some shit. Everyone knows what they don't like, it's quite simple, but I wanna give that now energy to what I like. I wanna get free.

PULL THE NET AWAY

You wanna see a tightrope walker not fall? Pull the net away. I don't believe in any net whatsoever. If you have a plan B you might use it, and that's not plan A. I don't mean you have to be sacrificed in plan A, I mean, 'Let's put all our thought and energy and let's break on through to the other side, let's use all the brain power we have to do it.'

CELEBRATE THE DIFFERENCE

Everyone says it's all one world and it's a small world. It's not. Have you ever tried to walk it? It's really big, actually. I think our differences are what is amazing. That's what we should celebrate, laugh at. I think the, sort of, taboo-ising of things annoys me about the modern world. I've always been a huge lover of comedy and comedians as being the philosophers of talking about what's difficult and finding ways to laugh at it. And so I don't like that people wanna regulate everything we say and do. I'm not a huge lover of the internet. I'm not really on it that much. I'd rather be living and I don't like anonymous activity like that.

LIFE IS HARD COS IT'S WORTH IT

I don't have the expectation for it to be easy or simple so I'm never let down by that. I'm around really eccentric, talented people that are really funny. When life is good it's funny and when life is bad, it's really funny. I got stung by a bee yesterday riding my motorcycle. I was dressed in bee-offensive dress. It was like a comedy, it stung a little, but it was funny, man. I was 'la la la' then 'argh!', it was hilarious, I don't mind that shit.

SHOW THEM WHERE YOU'RE FROM

It's not getting knocked down, it's getting up, that's where your style is. Whenever I get knocked down, I think, *well*, I'm gonna get up a certain way, and show them where we're from.

YP NOT AN MP

I was driving 90 miles an hour, totally safe in a modern car, on a modern road, and a detective pulled me over and he was so angry because I was from California and we were in Washington State. He was like, 'You're just a ... bonehead!' and I was like, 'Thank you, sir ... I know you're all upset. I can tell cos you're sweating. But forgive me for not giving a shit in the way you do about what you think. Sounds like a YP not an MP – your problem, not my problem. You're upset and I revel in that moment ... I'm from that place where I don't give a fuck what you think cos you're a cop. You think I'm supposed to dance? Jump? Run? Fuck that shit. You run if you're so adamant about it, my knee hurts. I don't run.'

Caleb Followill

Frontman, Kings Of Leon

*'I was a funny kid. I thought I was gonna
be a comedian when I was younger. I'd
annoy the shit out of people with it'*

USE YOUR IMAGINATION

I always loved looking out the window and it really gave me an
imagination. We never had money or anything but when I was
looking out the window, it was all mine. Every house I saw, that
was my house. Every time I saw something cool happening,
'Yeah, this is mine, I witnessed this.' I didn't drive for a long
time but now I love to drive and kind of have that moment
where I get to look around again.

LET IT HAPPEN

Most of the time if you hear a Kings Of Leon song on the radio
it's either *Sex On Fire* or *Use Somebody* or something from that

album. I look back with nothing but pride because there are a lot of people who've written a lot of songs and not many of them have that moment, had that song that goes that big and touches people all over the world. I'd be shocked if we ever had another song that was that successful. It's so fucking hard to tell with what's popular and what's not, I've pretty much given up on trying to figure out the mathematical equation. I think by trying to forget about that and stop doing that you end up accidentally writing another big hit. When I was writing *Sex On Fire*, I wasn't writing a hit, it just happened.

IF YOU DO SOMETHING WELL, DON'T DO IT FOR FREE

I was a funny kid. I thought I was gonna be a comedian when I was younger. I was Mr Chris Farley, Jim Carrey, whatever the newest comedian was, that's what I was doing. I'd annoy the shit out of people with it. I had a little bit of a ham in me. When I was little, I'd do stuff for $5. My mom would get $5 for me to do impersonations or for me to do a dance. I was a good-time kid.

DO IT FOR YOURSELF

With *Come Around Sundown* we did write stuff that was closer to home for us, we brought more country influence and stuff like that that we hadn't really touched on and maybe it alienated some of our fanbase a little bit. With *Mechanical Bull* we stripped it down even further and with *WALLS* we weren't trying to make arena-sounding songs, we were just trying to write songs that were great to us. And by the end of it, you listen to it and you're like, 'Ah!' We play it in our tiny little rehearsal space and they sound great in that room.

BIGGER ISN'T ALWAYS BETTER

Nowadays you see like these young acts that are doing 10 nights at Madison Square Garden and that kind of stuff, like Adele and Taylor Swift and those guys, so there's always something to reach for, not that we really wanted to do that. We're always happy to get the big pressure gigs like that over with and get to a smaller town where you can have fun. Somewhere that you don't have every person, record label person, people flying in to the shows, we're not really into that, it's too much pressure.

PITFALLS ARE PART OF THE PROCESS

Where do I start? I almost feel like you'd fuck yourself up too much if you did point out some pitfalls ahead. It's kind of good to go through it and experience it, fall down and get back up, fall down and get back up. It's how you grow.

BE REALISTIC

I've had some hard points. I've always been scared of massive success, so any time that's on the horizon and you can feel it and you can see from the people around you that something big is about to happen, those are always difficult times and that's when I go to a darker place. You've got to be positive and happy and be realistic about the fucking situation. We have a great life. When I was a kid, if I would've ever imagined the things that we've accomplished and the places I've been and the things I've seen. It's pretty unreal. Especially considering where we came from.

SURROUND YOURSELF WITH REAL FRIENDS

I have a lot of friends that don't pull any punches. They call it like they see it. And that's why they're my friends. I hang out with a lot of dudes that are 65 years old, I go and play golf with them and we go on little outings and eat good food and drink good wine, and those guys don't know anything about what I'm doing musically. They don't know anything. They don't even come to concerts, they're just my buddies. I get a lot of advice from them. And you learn about all the stuff that's happened to them in their 65 years sometimes makes you feel a little better about when you fuck up. It's important to see that and get that perspective.

LET GO OF YOUR GRUDGES

I'm very loyal to everyone around me. I can take a beating pretty good and still not be the kind of guy who will be mad at you for life. Usually whatever you're saying about me I've probably already said it to myself so I can understand why you're saying it.

DON'T TAKE SUCCESS FOR GRANTED

It's a great freedom we have to be able to wake up and decide that we want to make an album or we want to go out to the countryside and relax. It's not something we take for granted, we realise we're in a better position than almost every band in this town. There are a lot of bands out there who work a lot harder than us, they're carrying their gear into tiny venues that are half empty and trying to make it and they have jobs on the side. You can go to restaurants and your waiter has more talent than I could ever have but he just hasn't made it yet.

Big Boi

Rapper, Outkast

'I do dog shows, walking around the ring and all that. We won Best In Breed recently'

LEARN TO COMPROMISE

I've learned this from collaborating with other people. It's a good thing. Sometimes two minds are better than one. You get different perspectives, you can look at things from all angles and build off someone else's energy. It's like making a pot of stew. Someone is cutting up the celery, someone the carrots, the paprika, the pepper … When you want to make that special blend, you can only do it with the right ingredients.

BE ORGANIC

I don't believe in coincidences. All the energy you put into the universe comes back to you, so don't do something that's forced. A perfect example of being organic was working with

Snoop [Dogg]. When I first recorded the album he got on [new album *Boomiverse*], on the first song I worked on, I thought: 'Snoop would sound good on here.' Then just as I was about to turn the album in he did a listening party at my studio. It was organised at the last minute so I had to be somewhere else, but my engineer called me and said: 'Snoop's here and he wants to do a song with you.' I got him to play that first track and Snoop went: 'I'm not leaving till I've finished this one!'

GET A GOOD NICKNAME

I've had a few, yeah! The girls just started calling me Big Boi. I'd been doing a lot of push-ups so I've always been that brawny type guy, so it stuck. Then I've also got: Daddy Fat Sax, Sir Lucious Left Foot and The Knight In Rhyming Armour. The name has to be slick and embody some element of you. Left Foot is for my footwork, Lucious is real ghetto shit, and I'm from the 'hood. I gave myself a knighthood, but I'm the King now, for sure!

WHEN IT COMES TO DOGS:
QUALITY OVER QUANTITY

I've got a licence to breed pit bull dogs. I've always been an animal lover, so when I first got some money I invested in creating my own bloodline. That's where quality over quantity comes in. Pit bulls have a bad rep, but they're the sweetest dogs. When there's an issue, it's usually a pit bull mix, so I'm here to better the breed, promote the better traits. Do I do dog shows? Yes, the walking around the ring and all that. We won Best In

Breed recently. What's more competitive, dog shows or music awards? Dog shows!

BE TRUE TO THE REAL YOU

In a room full of carbon copies, it's important for you to be the original. There's only one you so don't be afraid to be you wholeheartedly! We got booed for being from the South when OutKast started out, but we stayed true. The Atlanta element in what I do is what I like to call 'elite street shit'. We're street-smart, book-smart guys who love what we do.

SHUFFLE

I'm always shuffling music and anything can come on. I've endless amounts of music. I can go from Sting to Kate Bush, to Beastie Boys to Bob Marley ... anything! I take inspiration from aspects of all genres. It's like a utility belt. They're all ingredients you can sample to make the toughest jams ever. Of course, if anything from Prince's *Purple Rain* or Michael Jackson's *Off The Wall* comes on I stop shuffling and listen to the whole album!

INVEST IN WHAT YOU KNOW

L.A. Reed [music industry mogul] taught me that. So, for example, from being in trailers on video shoots I had the idea to do my own. I started Big Boi Celebrity Trailers, and they're the plushest out there: marble floors, PlayStation, leather massage chairs ... it's an artist's home from home. It's doing really good.

... AND INVEST IN YOUR PEOPLE

I partnered on Celebrity Trailers with my old assistant and she's now a mogul in her own right! I always give my people a chance to climb the ladder. 'You're a young guy with a beat? Let's give it a go.' They call me the 'King of giving someone a shot'. My motto is: 'Be good to people.' Everything you put out comes back to you. That's how peace and love spreads all over the world, from people being good to people.

WHATEVER YOU'RE WEARING TODAY IS RIGHT!

Everything is right for the time. From the pink mink trousers at the [2001] MTV Video Music Awards, to the plaid '70s suit in [2003 OutKast single] *The Way You Move* video, they were classic pieces! We've got OutKast stuff in the [museum of US history] Smithsonian! Recently my wife got me into [yoga clothing company] Lululemon Athletica. They are so comfortable and breathable so I wear yoga tops and shit. It's right today!

LIFE IS ABOUT EVOLUTION

Always try to reinvent yourself, in a natural way. I'm always trying to find a new sound, new flows. Taking risks is the most important thing to me. I truly feel like my new record is a rebirth – it really feels like all bets are off. So actually my biggest Commandment or piece of advice for you is go get *Boomiverse*.

Chris Martin

Frontman, Coldplay

'You can do anything. Except win The X
Factor *twice, which I think is impossible'*

WAIT FOR THE BLESSING TO REVEAL ITSELF

I know a guy who's a suki and he said, 'You should check out
this poet Rumi.' When I read his poem, 'The Guest House', I
realised it was a completely different way of looking at life and
I realised that up to that point if I had a problem I'd try and
run away from it or medicate it or amputate it or be aggressive
against it. It's the fight or flight programme. But the concept of
this poem is, whatever's happening, if you sit with it, somehow
the blessing reveals itself. Even if it takes quite a long time.

PUT YOURSELF IN THE FIRING LINE

The whole journey of Coldplay is to be comfortable with being
in the firing line. I think what this journey has been about is

getting to the true core of what we do as a band and who we are as people and being proud of it. It was a really important journey to go on, to go, 'You know what? I'm in Coldplay and I also love them.'

FOLLOW YOUR CALLING

My true purpose is to be in this group. And through that we're able to get involved with things we really care about. I'd also love to be as gifted as a neurosurgeon, but that's not what I got given.

LIVE YOUR DREAM

All around you, you can see someone's dream come true, whether it's the person who wanted to design their house, or some boy from Devon who was like, 'I'd love to be in a great band', or the person right now who is making a cure for MS or something. Humanity is always moving forward with people dreaming ahead. You can do anything. Except win *The X Factor* twice, which I think is impossible.

REMEMBER TO SAY THANKS TO THE BOO-BOYS

Every person that's publicly been very vociferously anti what we're doing, they turn out to be blessings. Ten years ago we had someone in New York say we were the worst thing to ever happen to music. At the time I was like, 'God, why would they say that? That's really mean!' Now I'd be grateful to see that guy and say, 'Hey, thanks a lot, man.'

NEVER GIVE UP

The last words on *A Head Full Of Dreams* are, 'Never give up,' which is what my dad always says. And that's what I'm trying to say to myself. Sometimes you look at the world and think, 'Holy shit, there's too much to fix.' Or you can see that there's loads of people all the time coming up with great new things that make life and the world better. It's how you look at everything. You could watch the news and just give up.

TRIBALISM IS DEAD

I love pop music. I love listening to what my kids are listening to. I have as much fun listening to Ariana Grande and I love Nick Cave just as much. Coldplay are a product of all those other bands because we've grown up understanding that tribalism isn't as important in music as you used to think. You don't have to be just a goth or just a rocker.

LEARN FROM THE ELDERS

We've got the blessing of seeing *Westway To The World*, where Joe Strummer says, 'I wish we'd just taken six months off.' If you're in a younger band and watch that, you remember, 'If we're not getting along for a while, let's just take a break rather than announcing we split up.' When you look at A-ha, my favourite band as a teenager, it's great news to me that they reunited. You think, 'Why did you fucking break up in the first place?' It's seeing what Michael Stipe says about R.E.M.. We have all these teachers who say, 'If you wanna keep your band together, do this.'

THE WHOLE IS GREATER THAN THE SUM OF ITS PARTS

In a band where there's no virtuosos, the only thing you have is chemistry. The effect Brian Eno had on our band was extraordinary, picking up the confidence of the group, saying, 'What you need is within you.' On a musical level, you can do anything as long as no one is bothered if someone else says, 'We won't use that.' You've got to be free to experiment completely openly without being attached to whether everyone else wants to keep it or not.

REWARD BUSKERS

You've always got to reward a busker. That's one of my commandments. It's a hard job. Busking is fucking awesome. Like graffiti. Why don't people like graffiti?

Dave Gahan

Singer, Depeche Mode

'You don't have to be best mates. Life changes. It's about the music, it's not about the fucking individuals'

IT'S ALL OR NOTHING

All I really care about when I'm on the road is the show. How can I do my best performance? I'm old now, there's a lot of things I have to do, so I get up in the morning, I always wake up at like nine, drink a lot of water, get some food, eggs, then I start my routine. All I'm thinking about the gig which is coming at 9pm, get my head into that, stretch a bit, do a bit of yoga. You have to be all in, it's all or nothing. After all these years all I really want to do is perform to the best of my ability.

ENJOY IT WHILST IT LASTS

There was definitely a period when I was too out there to really appreciate how good it is. You don't appreciate it. One thing I've learnt and that I know right now is performing and stuff, this isn't forever. You've gotta enjoy it. It's amazing, it's fucking amazing. My favourite thing about it is, over all these years, all the shit that's been written and anything anybody believes or is between the band, it doesn't matter. It transcends everything, and I look out and I see the joy on people's faces. It's this amazing joy. I am fully aware that I'm living on borrowed time, it feels like. It's borrowed Depeche Mode time, or something. I'm appreciating it so much more than I ever have, I have a lot of fun with it and let go of any inhibitions I have onstage.

BLAG IF YOU NEED TO

I blagged my way into this band from the beginning. They were already a band before me – Vince, Fletch and Martin. They needed a front guy. I was an Essex lad. Vince thought he heard me singing *Heroes* by David Bowie in a rehearsal room next door with this other band. I was singing it, but so was a couple of other people too. We were all on the mic just jamming along. But when he asked me if that was me, I was like, 'That was me, yeah.' I had nothing else going on.

COLLABORATE WISELY

We were very lucky, we worked with some amazing people. We got a lot of really creative amazing people, all due to [label boss]

Daniel Miller. Full respect to Dan because if Daniel hadn't have found us and took us under his wing, God knows what would've happened. We would've been some awful fucking Spandau Ballet, Duran Duran-type thing.

DO YOUR OWN THING

When we first presented a couple of songs from [1986 album] *Black Celebration* to the radio plugger, it was fun to see. They were like, 'Where's the song for the radio?' We kind of realised that that was not our thing and by that time we'd created quite a following in Europe. They'd be places that we were respected for our albums. That was more important to us, making a body of work, making a piece of work.

PUT YOUR EGO TO THE SIDE

The ego stuff will always be there but the music is more important. You don't have to be best mates. Life changes. It's about the music, it's not about the fucking individuals. You realise that as you get older. You're not that important. There's something that happens, there's a chemistry. I remember Joe Strummer said once, the biggest mistake he ever made with The Clash was going along with the management and firing Mick Jones. They fired Mick from The Clash! Joe's great but you can't replace that. There's something between two guys . . . Jones and Strummer, Plant and Page, Gilmour and Waters. As a fan of music, I see it clearly, then I realised, that's what's going on with *my* band! It's me and Mart.

BE HONEST

Years ago, when me and my wife Jennifer first met, I was in this hospital or rehab in Arizona. I don't even know why she was there but it wasn't the same as me. We just started talking. She stayed there for a while and I stayed there for a few weeks. At the end, I remember saying, 'Let me get your number, we'll stay in touch.' She looked at me with this look, and said, 'Nah, we won't stay in touch.' It was one of the most honest things I'd seen for a long time. I was like 'you're probably right.' But funnily enough, she lived in New York and I lived in LA at the time and I went to New York months later and I got in touch with her and we became friends. I don't know. I was lucky. I've always been lucky like that in my life. People show up for me.

GET OUT OF YOUR COMFORT ZONE

You gotta go out of your comfort zone, gotta go out of what you do or who you are, to learn. One of the things with musicians, especially in bands, you get locked into this idea that that's who you are, that's your identity.

LOVE YOUR PETS

I lost my dog last year, she was a pain in the arse but amazing. I went on tour this year and my wife went out to a shelter and bought two more cats. Pets are amazing, they tell you a lot about yourself.

DON'T FORGET WHERE YOU'RE FROM

I wanted my kids to see where I grew up and we drove down to Basildon. I went back to that little house and the little bit of grass at the front and I was like, 'How did we all live in that little house?' Jimmy, my son said, 'So all that bit was where you lived?' I was like, 'No, that part there, that bit is *another house*. It's not one house. They are all joined together.'

Dave Grohl

Frontman, Foo Fighters

*'The day I get my face in a pile of cocaine is
the day that it all goes straight downhill'*

DON'T LET A BROKEN HOME BREAK YOU

My mom was a public schoolteacher; my dad was a journalist
and a speech-writer and PR guy. Y'know, we got by, but there
was no luxury. The luxury really was that we were happy. We
got by with very little and we were still the happiest people in
the world. [Their divorce] of course caused a lot of pain and a
lot of struggle. But I was six or seven years old and I don't think
I really understood what was going on. But then we settled into
this dynamic where we spent time with both parents. Both of
them were wonderful, intelligent, creative, musical people that
helped my sister and I learn to live happily.

THOU SHALT STEAL (IF IT'S FUNNY)

At [Sound City Studios in Los Angeles, making *Nevermind*] Kurt climbed up into the attic to jump down into the tape room where they had reels of tape from bands that had left them there over the years. One of the reels was an Evel Knievel tape. I guess Evel Knievel had made an album and so Kurt fucking stole it. I remember him walking out past the receptionist. He had that thing tucked into his long overcoat, like, 'OK, see you, bye'. He didn't even have a 24-track machine to play it.

BE PREPARED TO START OVER

My relationship [i.e. his marriage to photographer Jennifer Youngblood] broke up when we were making *The Colour And The Shape*. I didn't have anywhere to live, so I lived at my friend Pete's house in the [San Fernando] Valley. I literally had just a sleeping bag, a couple of pairs of pants. There's dogs peeing on my sleeping bag and six people living in this house. So I started looking for a place to live and I was driving with all my shit in the back of a U-Haul truck, coming up Laurel Canyon going into the Valley and I saw a sign that said House For Rent. That house was really important to me, because it was the first time that I just shed everything. I had to really start over. This was the birth of my independence.

SHARE THE PROFITS

At first, in Nirvana, all of the publishing was split evenly. It was all for one and one for all. And nobody thought what happened was gonna happen. So when it happened ... some things changed. Fuck, man, I'd never had a pay cheque bigger than $350. And all of a sudden you've got all that money floating around. And you think, 'Wow, I can live for the rest of my life off of what I've made this year.' So I didn't put up a fight. Because I didn't fucking care. Money and music don't necessarily meet. It's a tricky thing. The way I've always looked at it is that generosity and fairness goes a long way.

DON'T LET SUCCESS SPIN YOUR HEAD

It was probably after the Big Me video [in 1995] that I first got recognised. But it happened so gradually. Nirvana blowing up like a fucking fireworks display surprised everyone. But once you settled into that reality, it was such a gradual incline. I didn't get swallowed up in all of that bullshit. And God, man, I've seen so many people do it. I've seen so many people get eaten up by it. Or just fucking ... seduced by it. I can't imagine that it's easy to be seduced by something like that. But evidently it is.

IT'S OK TO TELL YOUR THERAPIST TO FUCK OFF

I remember talking about my problems to this therapist in Seattle once. The therapist was saying, 'Well, face it, you don't live in reality. You're flying around in jets, you're playing in front of thousands of people, you're shuttled from one place to the next.' And I said, 'Fuck you, motherfucker. Who are you to tell me what my reality is? You sit down and listen to people's problems all day. That seems a little fucking strange to me!'

TRY TO MEET YOUR HEROES

Neil Young is a hero of mine musically, but more so personally, just because he's a right-on guy. Bob Dylan is a gentleman, very cool. I met him in a hockey arena in Canada. He's got the hood up and he's leaning up against the wall, like a gunslinger. I said, 'Hey man, how's it going?' He's like, 'Hey, what's going on, Dave? Man, I really like that song Everlong.' I said, 'Really?' He goes, 'Yeah, I gotta learn that. I wanna start playing that.' I was like, 'Dude, you've got enough good songs. You don't need to fuck around with that.'

NEVER FORGET THAT COCAINE IS THE DEVIL'S DANDRUFF

I know that the day I get my face in a pile of cocaine is the day that it all goes straight downhill. I just fucking stay away from it. I'll never forget the first time I sat around a back lounge of a bus watching people do cocaine. I was just drinking. The first thing I noticed was that everyone was just talking out of their ass, talking fast about nothing. Nobody took their eyes off the fucking tray of cocaine. Urgh. It was just fucking weird. I was just looking at everybody like they were vultures. It just seemed dark and fucked-up to me.

ASK YOUR MOM ABOUT SOCIAL MEDIA

My mother had to explain Twitter to me. She usually can't even work a fucking remote control. So she explained it to me and I thought, 'What an incredible waste of fucking time. Get out of your fucking house and talk to someone to their face.' But then, the first tweet I wrote, I said, 'Dear Twitter, I take back everything I've said about you before. I didn't have an album to promote at the time.'

COUNT YOUR BLESSINGS

Everybody has their problems. I'm afraid to feel too good. But I count my blessings. I know that I'm the fucking luckiest man alive. And I feel that way every fucking day I wake up, man.

Eddie Vedder

Frontman, Pearl Jam

'Kurt Cobain and I were the same side of the coin - we were just different coins and one landed like that, and the other landed like that'

LET MUSIC BE YOUR SAVIOUR

I think I can speak for everybody in the group down to the last man that music's always been the most important thing in our lives and, so, if you ever get to the edge where you start losing it, then music, just like it helped you when you were 14, just like it helped you when you were 18, even now, decades later, it's still just the most important thing. It's like losing your wife, or the love of your life, you're not gonna fuck that up.

THE DRUGS DON'T WORK

Kurt Cobain and I were the same side of the coin – we were just different coins and one landed like that, and the other landed like *that*. It could be that random. Bill Hicks said, 'Not all drugs are good – some of them are great.' But you gotta know your way round them and my take on it is that some of them are horrible and once you delve into a certain kind of drug, you know the odds aren't good. I'm grateful that never really came across my path. I'd rather risk life and limb by trying to catch a 30-foot wave than stick a needle in my arm.

DON'T TURN YOUR BACK ON THE SEA

If you're a surfer, you don't turn your back on the water. There could be big waves on the horizon and if you're in the right spot you can catch those waves and ride 'em. If you're not, they're gonna land on your head. It's instinctual not to spend too much time looking back.

SHARE THE LOAD

Before, Pearl Jam felt like we were five little boats all tied together, now it feels like it's one big boat and we're all on it and we take turns at the wheel and we take turns in the engine room and we have a good understanding of being crew members and captains and sharing the load.

KEEP SHOVELLING THE COAL

I feel like success is fleeting, I still feel like you gotta be putting the coal in the fire, or however they ran the steam engines. You can't relax, you gotta keep shovelling coal.

ENJOY THE PROCESS

I wish I'd known a little earlier that it's more about enjoying the process of getting to where you're aiming to go, cos it's not about the destination, it's about the journey. When you're young, it's hard cos you're like, 'I wanna get there, what's round the corner, I wanna see what it's like ...'

PICK YOUR BATTLES

Taking on Ticketmaster, we got to see up close how things work in our country, we got to be crushed by a huge corporate giant right up close. It didn't kill us, but it was quite an experience and in some ways it robbed us of some of our idealism cos we thought and believed – and probably still do – that we were fighting the good fight. With longevity, you realise it's these spikes. If you can last long enough, if you can live long enough, these things that seem so important, they're just waves going up and down like a heartbeat on monitor. So if you can choose your battles, you don't have to have it threaten the life of the group, or your own life.

DON'T LOSE THE KID INSIDE YOU

Music does this thing where you're allowed to nurture part of yourself that was that committed kid when you were 10. I still get to enjoy the thing I've loved most, until I had a family, because of being in music. I can go and see shows and it not be like, 'Who's the fucking old guy?' I've got a reason to be there.

IT'S GOOD TO BE HUMBLED

There's a certain romanticism about surfing and it's all legitimate. These waves are coming from thousands of miles away and they get to the shore and explode like a firework and you're part of its existence. The power of experiencing water land on you, it doesn't care who you are or what you are. A three-metre wave, if it lands on your head, it's a real experience. Water's heavy! It's good to be humbled. In the winter in Hawaii, you're humbled on a daily basis. If you stop thinking about surviving for more than five or 10 minutes, you're gonna find yourself in trouble.

PUT YOUR PHONE DOWN

I think social media is a goddamn voicemail. If you've got voicemail and email, you're connected. If you need to go beyond that, then you might have some issues. You might have some attention deficit disorder. Needing attention. NADD. There's a lot of Naddists out there! Write a song or make art. That takes time and effort. I was playing these theatres and people were texting and when you're in a dark theatre, it looks like Avatar, light blue people.

Raekwon

Rapper, Wu-Tang Clan

*'You've got to study the greats in
order to be one of the greats'*

MIX IT UP, TRUST ME, I'M THE CHEF

I've been grilling a lot lately, making a lot of seafood on the
grill. I love fish ... and turkey burgers. We love turkey burgers.
People call me The Chef, not only because of my cooking and
my past [Raekwon's nickname 'The Chef' allegedly stems from
him making crack cocaine in his kitchen prior to joining Wu-
Tang Clan] but the different flavours of music I select to help
me become a better artist. The more you listen to timeless, great
music the more you become passionate about your music.

DON'T BE LAZY

There are a lot of lazy motherfuckers out there that want a lot
of shit to happen for them, but don't want to work for it. I'm a

full believer in working hard to receive your rewards. There's a saying that goes, 'He who works like a slave, eats like a king.' That is so fucking true. You gotta design yourself to be the best and go out there and want the best. That comes with putting in hard work and dedication.

DON'T BE A THIEF, BE A TAKER

I hate thieves. I don't like people who steal. I'd rather you'd take than steal. A person who takes something is more of a person I respect because he took it and he admitted it. A sneak thief is a person you could never ever trust and you never ever want to have around you. They do it because it's all they know. To me, you become the bottom of bottom, the lowest scum when you do shit like that. Don't be a thief, be a taker, y'know what I mean?

DON'T BE AFRAID TO SPEAK UP

In the Wu-Tang Clan I'm one of the outspoken ones in the group. I'm always going to say: 'I don't like that shit', or, 'That shit is dope.' It's all a way to protect what we built. I'm a firm believer in the team so when I spoke up I felt it was coming from a good spot. It ain't coming just cos I want to be heard. I saw things – great times ahead as Wu-Tang – and that was always behind my energy.

EDUCATE YOURSELF

Learning things is so important because we try to make a lot of analysis on our own without doing history or background checks on what makes sense. It's important to just know. You should do homework on stuff you love. You've got to study the greats in order to become one of the greats.

TAKE CARE OF YOUR HOME

Make sure you treat where you live like your kingdom. Don't shit where you sleep. We used to say back in the day you can't be a tough guy and do things right in your home because the trouble will come right back to your home. What's my home like? It's spotless, of course. I love the finer things, man.

KEEP BUSINESS AND FRIENDSHIP APART

When Wu-Tang was coming up we allowed ourselves to mix our friendships with our business, which wasn't really a great thing. We got burnt a lot from motherfuckers that really didn't have great intentions for us.

DON'T EVER STOP DREAMING

Don't ever give up on your goals and always be a true believer that dreams can come true. In the early days it was just the belief, the hope and the faith for us. It was one of the reasons why Wu-Tang Clan always had big expectations because we'd seen it in our minds. We felt that way, so we brought it into reality.

BE LOYAL TO THE PEOPLE THAT ARE LOYAL TO YOU

I'm so big on loyalty. Loyalty is more than money. When you're dealing with people who are dedicated to themselves and each other there's nothing that you can't get together.

KNOW YOUR BUSINESS

Any business you do, you need to be on top of. Don't ever take it for granted and always handle it the way you want it to be handled. You've got to be a good leader if you want your business to be what you want it to be. If you do that and follow everything else I just told you, everything will fall into place.

Matt Bellamy

Frontman, Muse

'We've lost faith in ourselves, we're putting more faith into robots and machines and the efficiency of computers'

BRING SOMETHING NEW

The band has been on this, for want of a better term, progressive journey, sort of testing how far we can go. It's just the three of us, guitar, bass and drums. Up to the third album, we really focused in on that and made it work really well, the three-piece thing, trying to bring something new to what is essentially old, established instruments. There's been some great, very clever, very talented people over the last few decades that have used those instruments to make music. It's always a challenge to come in using just guitar, bass and drums and try and to do something new.

BE DEDICATED

My life went through a difficult twist when I was a teenager and that's what led me to be in a rock band and it made me really focus, put everything into music. My parents broke up when I was a teenager. That was around the time that looking back on it now, I was just like, 'Whatever, I'm joining a band, I'm joining my mates, we're going on tour,' and I guess in some ways the band became a family. At the time, it wasn't like I didn't feel sadness or anything but I became so obsessed with the music. I was so into that the music itself had a nature of expression to it that kind of revealed what was going on in my life.

TAKE STOCK WHEN THINGS GO WRONG

You think you have an idea of what your life is and then it's gone and something changes and it shifts and you have to reinvent, you have to restart basically, and that's happened to me about three or four times in my life. It happens to everybody, everybody goes through these things. When I look at all those times it's happened in my life, whether it be teenage years or other points, you think, 'Where am I and what am I doing?' It was a little bit of self-discovery and redefining who you are.

TECHNOLOGY DOESN'T ALWAYS MEAN PROGRESS

We know there's two sides to the sword, whenever there's a new technology around. They've invented these autonomous killing machines, so in other words, these drones that can make their own kill decisions. It's obviously wrong because I feel like human empathy is in decline and I think the technology is one of the main components of that. All the different things that humans can do are essentially being redone more efficiently by machines, and definitely with zero emotion. We've lost faith in ourselves, we're putting more faith into robots and machines and the efficiency of computers.

KEEP YOUR FRIENDS CLOSE

There's moments where you can lose your head a little bit. You get so surrounded by these weird hanger-on types, they're everywhere, especially out in LA, random people that are just looking to use you for something. There's a lot of that going on, trying to push stuff on you. There is a dark side and a lot of people can fall foul of that. The good thing with the guys in the band is that when we get in a room together and start playing music and just chatting and mucking about and laughing and stuff, we have a sort of immunity to the darker side of what the industry can offer. I think we've kept each other in check, and we've been there for each other.

LET THE GOOD TIMES ROLL

The lowest point in the band was when I was drinking more than I should have, and I ate an entire chorizo sausage in Spain and woke up in the middle of the night in the bunk just covered in sick. I got up in the bus, it was like three in the morning, and realised there was no shower, I had no real change of clothes, they were all sweaty and dirty, and I had to sit like that and smell like that for at least six hours and then try and do a gig. I came back from that tour and said, 'If we don't start having a good time, I don't really wanna do it.' So when we did the second album, it was all about having a good time.

DON'T TAKE YOURSELF TOO SERIOUSLY

The second album was the biggest laugh ever, I remember laughing non-stop for about a year because we stopped taking ourselves so seriously, we stopped trying so hard, we just wanted to have a good time all the time. Musically it changed because of that, everything changed, the way we were onstage changed. Everything got a bit more fun, it got more ... I think that's why we're still here because we made that decision not to mope around.

NAP WHEN YOU CAN

When you have a kid you just get used to not having much sleep. What I've learned to do is how to have a powernap. At four o'clock in the afternoon, I can literally go down for 15 minutes and feel great. I do that a lot now. It's taught me the art of the nap.

GET OUT AND EXPLORE

We did a concert in Iceland so while we there, we thought, 'We might as well go on a trip', so we went into the inland area, a few hours' drive away from Reykjavik. We went to all the volcanic areas, places where there's no people around for miles and miles.

We climbed mountains, we went into lava caves. Also, it was a chance for me to really learn how to become a drone pilot cos there's no regulations there at all so I could just fly the drone and discover all these amazing things. Some of those things I don't think have ever been filmed before. There's one waterfall and it was in the middle of nowhere and no one has filmed it before and it doesn't have a name. I felt like I was Attenborough. If this all doesn't work out, I'd love to be a drone cameraman. When you have a couple of days off, you've got to explore. That's the whole point of touring.

EMBRACE THE ONESIE PARTY

For anybody who wants to experience something that is truly of our time, something that will be looked back upon in terms of, 'I can't believe that happened', Burning Man festival is in that category. It's just wild. It's crazy, it's a massive costume party, everyone is nice to everyone, it feels safe, it's the safest place you could ever be, it's also the wildest place you could ever be. My favourite moment was when we went to a onesie party, so we dressed up in little onesies. I was a tiger and we had little hooks on our tails, we danced around. You don't need to take any drugs to be fucked there, what you see and what you experience is enough to make you go, 'What is happening in the world, this is so different to anything in reality?'

Matthew Healy

Singer, The 1975

'I cry a lot. If I say stuff like, "I'm a really sensitive soul", I genuinely mean it. Fucking hell, put on Finding Nemo or All Dogs Go To Heaven, I cry'

HOME IS WHERE THE ART IS

Home for me, from when I was 14 onwards, was The 1975 hub, so my garage. Everything orientated from there. If I was there, I knew at one point during the day somebody was going to come round, everything was based out of there. That's why tourbuses are kind of home for me. As long as I'm writing and stuff, that's what is home for me.

IT'S ALL RIGHT TO BE ON YOUR OWN

I'm this massive extrovert onstage, but I'm genuinely quite an introverted person. I'm becoming a bit of a hermit. So there's part of me, I'm a bit like, 'I shouldn't be like that. I'm 27, winning

Brits and stuff.' There's this weird kind of polarity between like me turning up to the Brits all glitzy and doing a performance and coming straight home and feeding the dog and being in bed by one in the morning. That's who I am, and I've had to accept that, that it's all right to like being on your own. I come from getting stoned in my bedroom and writing music and that's what I really enjoy doing.

JUST BECAUSE THEY DID IT DOESN'T MEAN YOU HAVE TO

I look at pictures, like the history of rock'n'roll, and I see everybody out together at parties and I think, 'Fucking hell, maybe I should be doing that', because I feel maybe a cultural duty to do that, but I don't really want to.

SNAKE, EMAIL, TEXT AND RING IS ALL YOU NEED

Have you seen Nokia are bringing out the 3310 again? I'm buying one. Because what have you got? Snake. Email. Text and Ring. That's all I need, that's all I want.

THERE'S NO SPACE FOR NOTHINGNESS

Pop music can be didactic, to use a word that's a bit wanky but purposely informative. A song can be about anything as long as it's about something. Stuff that just rhymes needs to go. Songs like *Radioactive* by Imagine Dragons. It might as well be called *Pikachu Banana*. It's nothingness. There's no space for nothingness any more and pop music has so much space for it.

SEEK OUT INSPIRATION

I listen to a lot of my own music. Not in a narcissistic way, but I've always been fearful of over-referencing other artists. I'll let stuff breathe and then I'll listen to stuff of ours and I try and take an inspiration from it. A lot of the time, I'm feeling imposter syndrome, like I'm gonna get rumbled, I'm doing something that isn't good enough. There's a brilliant Brian Eno quote, 'Inspiration isn't gonna come looking for you.' As an artist you do that, sitting at a thing waiting for it to come to you. That's not what happens, it's after three hours on the same synth sound, fourth cup of coffee and nothing, and then one thing happens that's a bit different and then that literally opens up a door.

BE THE BOSS

It's been important for me, being on an indie label [Dirty Hit]. I'm not just the singer in The 1975, this is my whole thing. I'm sure I feel more responsibility than other artists do because this is my vision that is being auteured so it's not something I can give to a committee. It's made me feel good, cos I get to be this creative person that lives in an eclectic place with lots of stuff going on, making music and having a slightly decadent life, but I am also responsible for the careers of a lot of people and that's also something I take really seriously.

IF YOU NEED TO HAVE A BIG CRY, HAVE A BIG CRY

I cry a lot. But not in an indulgent way. When I get that moment and I've just nailed it, it makes the hairs on my neck stand up. And if I wanna cry, then I try to. Or I let it happen. I know that sounds really self-indulgent but it's important to me because it portrays how much value music has to me. Because I'm a really sensitive soul. It's difficult for me to be genuine in print. If I say stuff like, 'I'm a really sensitive soul', I genuinely mean it. Fucking hell, put on *Finding Nemo* or *All Dogs Go To Heaven*, I cry. I cry at films on planes. I cry at films all the time, but for me it's a way of validating how much I feel about something.

EMBRACE YOUR LIMITATIONS

There's an emotional fragility behind formulaic songwriting that is simple and resonates with people. Musically-minded people make awful music and culturally-minded people make brilliant music. If you're too good a musician you become slightly more self-indulgent or more interested in your own musicality as opposed to it being a vehicle for a message. You become wanky. I love music and I'm a musicphile but I'm not the best musician in the world so I think my limitations mean that I have to better myself or compete by giving a humanity that isn't there with other pop music. I have to give a bit of myself, or my lyrics have to be better or my message has to be stronger to allow the simplicity of our music to translate.

FIND VALUE IN REAL THINGS

That's what makes me happy. My family make me happy. One of the things you struggle with when you go on tour is the management of, not your relationships with the people you tour with because that's just diplomacy – we've been together for 15 years so that's easy – it's being there for people and valuing certain things.

Neneh Cherry

Singer

'I've been known to have a few problems with rage'

TAKE A TIME-OUT DURING DOMESTIC DISPUTES

My husband and I had a little domestic a couple of weeks ago. I slammed a few doors, fell apart, went out for a walk around the block and lit a fag. I was feeling completely misunderstood but, amazingly, by the time I'd come back, everything was fine!

DON'T GO LOOKING FOR 'BAD SHIT' ON SOCIAL MEDIA

I read my Twitter a little bit most nights. Usually people say nice things on it and I don't go searching for the bad shit. There's always a few haters, but, yeah, I'm trying to keep my eye on the ball of the *nice* things.

GET YOUR BEST FRIEND TO COOK
AT YOUR DINNER PARTY

Recently I moved back to London from Sweden and I was at
my best friend Andrea's kitchen in a pub where we hosted a
Thanksgiving dinner for 70 people. How about that? She made
this amazing kind of maple/ale syrup served in a funny plastic
bucket – it looked like it'd come out from underneath somebody's bed in a prison cell! It was delicious though.

SING WHEN YOU'RE DRIVING

My daughter Mabel and I always sing along to a lot of
Frank Ocean in the car. To me, he's a great poet of where
we are, here and now. Also Alice Coltrane has kind of re-
emerged back into my life through my daughters [listening
to her]. She was always a sort of spiritual, healing force in
my upbringing. I've also been listening to a lot of her grand-
nephew, Flying Lotus. It's so interesting hearing her universe
in his music.

RAGE AGAINST BULLSHIT LOGIC

I had an 'anger attack' – I've been known to have a few problems with rage – while I was checking in for a European flight
last summer when we were doing the festivals. We had an
argument about me being allowed to take two bags on board
as hand luggage. They were both small enough to put under my
seat, but they insisted I put one inside the other because it was
supposedly safer and quicker or whatever. I hate the bullshit

logic of it! I just wanted to get on the plane and have a calming drink and read my book.

JUDGE A MAN BY HIS LOOKS

The last person on Earth I'd want to spend time with is Putin. Oh Jesus fucking Christ! I don't have a lot of good feelings about that man. I don't like the way he looks, his hair, what he thinks, what he says ... I don't want to be near him!

DON'T PRETEND YOU'RE DANGEROUS IF YOU'RE NOT

I don't break the law very often. Maybe jaywalking was the last time. But I wouldn't tell if you had, probably because it's something totally boring and wouldn't make me sound dangerous. Which I'm not! If I'm honest, it'd probably be a little scam I did somewhere, pocketing something for cheap.

VIVE LA DIFFERENCE

I've definitely been in Sweden and wished it was a bit more like London or New York. But I think the beauty of different places is what they are, rather than wanting them to be like other places. But then, like maybe on a Monday morning in London in the pissing rain going down into the Tube I've thought, 'God, I wish my phone would work and it wasn't so fucking dirty down here.'

STAY CLEAR OF RIGHT-WING POPULIST POLITICS

The rise of UKIP over here was depressing and scary, but also an incredible insight into the sign of our times. Unfortunately, it's a temperament that's not just happening here, it's all over Europe. It gives me the heebie-jeebies.

EMBRACE THE AGEING PROCESS

I recently turned 50. Time freaks me out a bit. It's fast. Much faster than I am, so that's slightly disturbing. But I don't regret. It's a pointless exercise. I can't change getting older so I just try to embrace it.

Suggs

Singer, Madness

*'My underwear was blowing around
Bowie's drive and there he was, the great
man, picking up my socks and vests'*

STAY TRUE TO YOUR NICKNAME

My mum still calls me Graham. She's like, 'Suggs, Spuds,
Smudge . . . whatever it is. I gave you a perfectly good name and
it's faintly ridiculous to be called that when you're a 56-year-old
man!' But Suggs is who I am and I've done all right by it, so I'm
sticking with it.

LOOK BEYOND WHAT PEOPLE SAY

I bumped into Morrissey two years ago at some awards ceremony. It was very brief and he was very friendly, as much as he
can be anyway. I don't dig a lot of what he says, but I like his

work. He says a lot of outrageous things, but often I think it's just Morrissey being Morrissey.

KNOW WHAT A BOMB LOOKS LIKE

I really got the fear a few months ago when we dug up a German 500kg bomb [for TV show WW2 *Treasure Hunters*] in the marshes around Merseyside. I'm no expert in tangled metal stuff, but I quickly recognised this big, bomb-shaped thing coming out of the ground. We're just about to run when the director goes, 'Can you just do a little piece to camera?' and I was like, 'Er, not unless we do it five kilometres away!'

NEVER USE YOUR FAME TO GET
PREFERENTIAL TREATMENT

I have never said, 'Do you know who I am?' to get in somewhere. But I do remember being outside a nightclub once and hearing Billy Idol say exactly that. Everyone around him was rolling around on the floor laughing. So I've always been wary of that sort of outcome.

DON'T MIX ALCOHOL AND POLITICS

Recently we were trundling around northern Europe in our tourbus and one night we'd had a few cold drinks and we started talking about politics. Suddenly it all went a bit hay-wire: 'Fake news this, fake news that . . .' I ended up arguing with pretty much everyone and anyone.

BE WARY OF PUTTING YOUR LUGGAGE ON THE ROOF RACK

There's this famous incident when I went with our producer Clive Langer to visit David Bowie's home in Gstaad, Switzerland. We just happened to be driving past with our families on holiday and we turned up with all our suitcases on the roof and there he is in the garage, the Starman. And just as we drove in we heard this loud crunch and my suitcase came flying off the roof and my underwear was blowing around Bowie's drive and there he was, the great man, picking up my socks and vests ... it wasn't the first impression I was hoping for! He was a very, very charming man. I think he's one of the last of those people who can engender that sort of enigma because when you met him he wasn't like that at all, he was actually very down to earth.

DON'T BE AFRAID OF PULLING AN ALLNIGHTER

Every now and then I'll stay out all night, usually at either Trisha's or Gerry's in Soho, London. Just the very mention of the name Gerry's and you know you've got on the wrong side of the alarm clock.

NEVER COUNT YOUR CHICKENS ...

My recent show *What A King Cnut* is about what happens to you when you get famous. Showbusiness is a fickle thing, and you constantly think someone's going to tap you on the shoulder and ask you what you're doing here. Fame is a tightrope and it is very easy to fall off.

KNOW THE LAW OF THE LAND

I don't make a point of breaking the law, but at the moment I'm smoking in this hotel room in Butlins, Minehead. I'm not sure whether or not that's actually breaking the law, but I'd imagine there might be some sort of punitive fine for it or something.

STARE THE APOCALYPSE DOWN
WITH A BAG OF CHIPS

In my current situation, should the end of the world happen right now, I'd probably go for a swim in the sea, get a bag of chips then spend a couple of hours at Billy Butlin's funfair.

Richard Ashcroft

Singer, The Verve

*'They're a cut-throat group the ex-footballers.
You don't break into their turf easily, man'*

YOU CAN TAKE THE BOY OUT OF THE NORTH ...

I miss the general interaction you get in shops in the North. Getting called 'love' when I'd go to the chip shop as a kid. If I was buying chips, in that process I'd get called love about six times. You think it's just throwaway but actually you miss it when it's not there. 'You all right there, love? You want salt and vinegar with that, love? Do you want a bit of pea wet on that, love?' 'Mate' just isn't the same.

SING IN YOUR OWN VOICE

It's good to see grime and that side of our music culture really representing on a global scale now. I'll be listening to a radio station and there might be three American rappers on and then a London voice comes on and it's really refreshing. That colloquial thing has become massive. People want to hear people from their turf talking in their slang. I love all that.

DON'T READ YOUR OWN PRESS

Me and Kate [Radley, wife] were in bed the other night and she showed me a review of my gig at the O2. I see a guy who doesn't understand what I do and he writes something like 'keyboard squiggles' about [solo track *Out Of My Body*]. *That's* the way they analyse one of the greatest songwriters this country has ever produced? Unless you're that indie fantasy, unless the writer thinks him and Thom Yorke are going to go off to Antarctica and record a reindeer mating call album with Aphex Twin. Unless it's in that field, you just don't get the same thing. I don't know whether it's a class thing or whatever.

FOOTBALL PUNDITS ARE A CUT-THROAT BUNCH

I could have been a professional footballer but now at my age I would be looking for a spot on *Question Of Sport* or something. Gary Lineker's boxed everything off *and* he's doing the crisps, do you know what I mean? It's tough to break in. They're a cut-throat, almost Masonic-like group the ex-footballers. You don't break into their turf easily, man.

MIX UP YOUR 'DO

My mum was a hairdresser and she used to try out new styles on me. I had something different nearly every Friday night. There's not many styles I haven't tried. I accidentally shaved it all off once. I'd put the clippers on zero without realising it. I put it up the back and went bald straightaway so I tried to make it a bit better … Kate came downstairs and I was stood in the lounge completely bald.

CROSS-POLLINATE

It was great when Noel Gallagher wrote *Cast No Shadow* about me. I was buzzing. I was thinking more cross-pollination could have gone on at the time, we could have really consolidated our thing. In hip-hop culture they completely got it, what they had with their own culture. We [in the UK] need to do things together and realise what we've got because we're in the DNA of the greatest country in the world for rock'n'roll.

TAKE WHAT CHRIS MARTIN SAYS
WITH A PINCH OF SALT

Chris Martin called me 'the best singer in the world' but he says a lot of things. I heard him say that Supergrass were the greatest band in the world at a gig once. I mean, Supergrass are a good band but that obviously shows he's prone to exaggeration.

REMEMBER WHERE YOU COME FROM

I heard Peter Sellers used to say 'Not today' when people asked him if he was Peter Sellers in the street. That doesn't really sit well with me. If someone recognises me and wants a picture I'm happy to oblige because making that journey to work on a rainy day in Wigan every day was so bad that I never ever want to return to that. Not that I'm going to be forced to do that again, but I never want to return to that place in my mind, so I'm happy for each individual person who has helped me get one little tiny step away from that.

HAVE AN OPINION

We miss people with opinions. Whatever it is, at least have a fucking opinion. People don't have opinions. Unless they think they're going to get PC credits for it, then they're out there – oh man – appeal after appeal, they're out there holding babies and making everyone feel really guilty around Christmas.

BE A ROCK'N'ROLLER 24/7

I had a big old white Mercedes 1969 convertible and was coming home from the studio at four in the morning and a dude in a van saw me. He beeped his horn and gave me a big fist out the window. I thought. 'I'm buzzing that he saw that.' You'd think he'd be like, 'You fucking bastard . . .' In rock'n'roll we've lost that, the pink Cadillac and all that shit. The hip-hop lads know, but we're scared to be a rock'n'roller and live our lives. Live it, and make it a movie.

50 Cent

Rapper

*'When I recorded Wanksta I didn't know what
wanker meant in the UK. Afterwards they
told me I was like, "Oh shit, hold on…"'*

BE A BALLER, NOT A BASEBALL PLAYER

I totally missed when I tried to throw the first pitch at a New
York Mets game last season. Afterwards I was like, 'Yo, can I do
it again?' I ain't going to lie, there was so many people looking at
me, it's like, 'The fuck just happened, man?' I'm trying to throw
the ball hard and get a fast strike in front of everybody, then the
shit slips out of your hand. They got fucking collectors' baseball
cards of it. Public domain my ass, that's my image! That's one
of the pictures I would like taken down.

PARTY LIKE IT'S YOUR BIRTHDAY

When it's my birthday I enjoy myself. This year I went from [nightclubs] Orbit in New York to Ace Of Diamonds in Los Angeles. I started on the fourth [of July, two days before his birthday] and just went on through. It's all a celebration. You should celebrate every day until the next one!

I'M NO BOXING EXPERT

I took part in the Junior Olympics as a boxer but when I was in [boxing film] *Southpaw* in no way did I present myself as a boxing expert. Jake [Gyllenhaal, actor] did a great job, he really slimmed himself down. I had to put on weight for my role. I had the luxury of cookies. I enjoyed myself. While he was going through intense training, I was having cookies and cake and shit.

WRITING MUSIC IS BETTER
THAN SELLING CRACK

If I could go back in time to talk to myself when I was 12 years old [the age he started selling drugs on the street] I wouldn't have even started hustling. I would have told him to start making music back then. I'd be so much better now because I'd have been writing music since I was 12. I would have had a head start!

CHECK YOUR SLANG

When I recorded the song *Wanksta* for the *8 Mile* soundtrack I didn't know what it meant in the UK. Afterwards they told me what a wanker was. I was like, 'Oh shit, hold on . . .' It does fit with the song, though. Would I have called the song that if I knew what it meant? Probably not!

DON'T TURN THE LIGHTS OFF
IN MIKE TYSON'S HOUSE

I bought a house off Mike Tyson in Connecticut that had 52 rooms. I tried to go into every room and feel out the place. I took two days; it's like a small hotel! I wouldn't turn the lights off. When you've got a 52-room place, when you don't use shit they break because you didn't use it, so you leave the fucking lights on!

DON'T LOSE YOUR BOTTLE

When I got bottled off at Reading Festival in 2004 it was fun. Look, they did that to everybody. That shit was crazy! We all just started throwing shit. They was throwing shit, we was throwing shit back. Everything that could be thrown off the stage that couldn't be tied down. At first, it was water bottles and stuff like that. Y'all don't want to be hit by a water bottle because they've been out there so long that that's not water. They threw shit at everybody who came up there. I don't care who you were, you went out there and they threw shit at you. They would have thrown some shit on Michael Jackson, it didn't matter.

MONEY DOESN'T IMPRESS EMINEM

I flew from LA to Detroit to talk to Eminem about a movie. It was a film where we were supposed to be playing two guys from different sides of the tracks. I'm the head of this gang in Detroit and he's the head of another gang. His thing was he didn't like to leave Detroit. So I said, 'Hey, they want to give you eight million dollars to do it and we don't have to leave Detroit, so you can go home every night!' He read the synopsis and was like, '[Furrows brow] It's cool but we should do something like [cult '70s New York gang film] *The Warriors.*' I said, '*The Warriors?* What the fuck, Em? *The Warriors?* Did you just hear me say they want to give you eight million dollars and you don't have to leave Detroit?' He didn't give a fuck.

INVEST, INVEST, INVEST

I get asked to invest in a lot of different stuff. People wanted me to get involved in making fuel from garbage. Where you burn the garbage and turn it into fuel. Biofuel, that kind of stuff. Some of it [the world of energy companies] is so sophisticated, it feels crazy how far you can get into the way the world works.

BE THE BOW

Surviving a murder attempt makes you reassess life. When you get hurt that bad it makes it clear that you're not in control. After something like that happens, either your fear consumes you or you become stronger. If you give me a fucked-up situation, I'll give you a good one afterwards. I am the bow: you may see me pulled back at points but it's only so I can shoot forwards faster than you've seen me shoot forwards before.

Noel Gallagher

Singer/songwriter, Oasis

*'I couldn't be a judge on The X Factor.
I would just end up saying to Louis
Walsh, "Will you shut up, you c**t"'*

IF YOU MAKE GOOD RECORDS,
NOTHING ELSE MATTERS

It doesn't matter that I'm a shit frontman and some nights I
don't say anything. The razzmatazz and the fucking jujitsu and
the Mick Jagger and all that shit people get up to. That's amazing, don't get me wrong, but what I've got is songs that people
genuinely want to sing. Someone wrote: 'Noel as a frontman is
a work in progress.' What does that fucking *mean?* A work in
progress? What do they think I'm doing now, down the gym
in front of a mirror with a Telecaster going, 'Yeah, if I could do
some lunges in this bit that'd be great. Maybe I should wear
bigger heels?'

LAURELS ARE THERE TO BE RESTED ON

I'm too bone idle to be like Damon Albarn. That guy? Fucking hell. I was saying to him, 'Have you *ever* had a month off? I used to be like that but I do like resting on my laurels. Every time I think about going back to work *AKA … What A Life!* will come on the radio and I'll go, "Haha, what's the point? Fucking done it. Going to the Groucho, see you later."'

BEING THE LEAD SINGER IS EXHAUSTING

Being a singer, you go onstage and then before you know it, you're announcing the last song. You've got to be so on it. Whereas in Oasis I was like one of the fans. I was just singing the odd backing vocal thinking, 'This is fucking *mega*.' I didn't really have anything to do in an Oasis gig for 40 minutes. Now you've got to be on it from the first song to the last. It takes up so much mental energy. You come offstage and people go, 'Wow, that was great!' and you're like, 'Was it? I have no fucking idea, can I have a banana?'

NEVER DO *THE X FACTOR*

They asked me to be an *X Factor* judge. I think they think that because my tour's finished I'm going to be bored, but I'm never going to be *that* bored. Sharon Osbourne gets £1.5 million for doing it I've heard. If she's worth one and a half, what am I worth? Three? Three and three-quarters? I've not got anything against the show, I just don't want to be on the telly every Saturday night, fuck that. You may be aware, I've got a slight

case of Tourette's syndrome and I would just end up saying to
Louis Walsh, 'Will you shut up, you c**t!'

DON'T ALWAYS TRUST PAUL WELLER'S TASTE

I don't listen to the radio any more, I'm really reliant on Paul
Weller. I don't know what he does, he must listen to independent radio all the time because he's forever on the phone to me
saying, 'Have you got this? Check this out, check that out.'
Most of it is shit. But he's still getting in there, do you know
what I mean?

KNOW WHEN TO BOW OUT

Imagine if Oasis had walked offstage at Knebworth and that
had been it. It would have been the greatest story of all time. A
better story than The Beatles, Elvis, all of that shit. But we were
too caught up in the thing. You're like, 'Fuck this, we'll come
back next year and do five fucking nights!'

YOU'LL NEVER LIKE MEXICAN FOOD
AS MUCH AS CHRIS MARTIN

If you think Chris Martin is an excitable chap about music, I
can only tell you that I've never seen a man get so excited about
a Mexican food order in my life. He got so excited about this
Mexican meal we were about to have in LA once. He was fucking mental for it.

THE INTERNET IS ACTUALLY SHIT

No one's telling me that, as great as the internet has been, it's a cause for good. It's spread evil and shitness and it's taken away magic, and everyone knows everything about everybody. Modern life's shit. I don't find it sexy, romantic, magical. It's not inspiring in any way.

... BUT DOWNLOADING MUSIC IS FINE

I download music. Where do you buy records these days? I can't go to HMV. How long do you think it would take me to get out of HMV if I went in? If I go into a record store they usually turn into autograph sessions so I avoid them now.

DON'T GET THE BAND BACK TOGETHER

I don't need the money, I don't need the glory, I don't need to relive the memories. If I was to get Oasis back together tomorrow and then do a tour, I'd have a hundred million dollars in the bank but I'd have learnt fuck-all. I'd have actually wasted a year. I could understand it if we were a band who'd been going for five years and were just at our peak, but Oasis have got no unfinished business. We did it. We fucking did it, and then some. It's done.

Ed Sheeran

Singer-songwriter

*'I am living proof that people
are not born with talent'*

DON'T DRINK (OR SMOKE WEED) ON THE JOB

We don't have booze in the venue until after the gig. I love embracing chaos, but only when the job's done. I worked really hard to get into this position and I'm going to continue working hard to maintain the position and grow. And I've stopped smoking weed, I found myself just sitting at home watching films. I only ever create sober, I like to be alert. I find most ideas happen when you have a cup of tea, for me anyway.

ACCEPT YOUR PALENESS

We can't all get away with spray tans. I'd look weird with a spray tan. I am myself, with freckles. A lot of people in Britain are very pale like me. Especially gingers. Find me a tanned ginger, it's not gonna happen!

YOU DON'T HAVE TO RUN ON VENGEANCE

I don't write songs from a vengeance point of view. I never think, 'I'm going to get this person back.' I've never woken up and thought, 'OK, let's book Wembley Stadium because cool journalists don't like me.' I'm saying, 'Let's book Wembley Stadium because I want to play it and I want to sell it out.' It's not to rub it in anyone's face, who didn't believe in me. Although sometimes it does rub in people's faces.

BEING A CARTOON IS A WINNER

Any artist that's big you can draw a caricature of them, or even an outline, and everyone knows who it is. You can just draw Serge from Kasabian's hair and you know it's Serge. That's when you're onto a winner and with me it's red hair. It's nice that it's the thing that got me noticed because I was ribbed about it at school. Parents with ginger children come up to me and go, 'It's now cool to have ginger hair.' That wasn't the case years ago. Everyone loves Prince Harry and Rupert Grint. The ladies love Grint.

BEING ENGLISH HELPS IN AMERICA

Being English goes a long way in Hollywood. In any situation, I benefited from it. Not sexually, professionally! Americans think we're kooky and fun. When I lived there I was in all these situations, dinner parties, clubs, meeting people and thought, 'All this could end tomorrow, I better do it all now so I'll at least have some decent stories.' I definitely lived it. I did everything that I should've done. And everything I shouldn't.

BEING WEIRD SETS YOU UP FOR LIFE

I was a weird kid. I had a massive birthmark round my eye, had to get it lasered off, which fucked my retina, and I have a lazy eye. That's why I hate red carpet photos, there's always one where there's an eye going … over there. I had NHS glasses, a wonky eye, a stutter and a missing ear drum. I couldn't swim unless I wore sports goggles which had a flicky thing at the top which everyone said was a penis. All the cool kids in primary school aren't doing a lot now and I've come out of it a hit. My view on it is God looked down one day and was like, 'Fucking hell, you need some help, mate, here's a guitar.' I'm glad I had all that and I appreciate it now. It rounded me as an individual.

DON'T BE A MUG

As soon as I signed my publishing deal, before I got big, I bought property. I've invested in three in England. I think pop stars nowadays are just more sensible. Because it doesn't last as long. It's all about: do your time, earn your money, buy some property and when it all goes to shit you've got something to fall back on. The guy that told me to buy property was Goldie. I met him when I was 17, he kept in touch and as soon as stuff started to go well he rang me up and goes, 'Don't be a cunt, buy a fackin' "aaahse!".'

EVERYONE'S A GEEK ON THE INSIDE

I attract the outsiders, who find solace in music. Kids turn up to my shows on their own. Music attracts the awkward person in all of us. We live in a world which tries to make you conform to 'perfection'. No one is perfect. *Everyone's* a geek. In some way. We are *all weird*.

HARD WORK GETS YOU EVERYWHERE

Persistence gets you wherever you want to go. My dad always said, 'Nothing ventured nothing gained.' It was never 'It either works or it doesn't,' you don't stop until it works, basically. I applied that to the [2014 single] *Thinking Out Loud* video, I was rehearsing five hours a day thinking, 'Why the fuck am I learning to dance? I make the music, someone else can dance.' But I set out to do it and I did it. If you feel like you should do something but it's a risk, just fucking *do it*. If it's positive, obviously. Don't do anything bad!

LEARN YOUR CRAFT

I started off with zero talent, I couldn't sing, I couldn't play guitar. I am living proof that people are not born with talent. I've had to learn my craft.

Mad Professor

Producer and dub icon

*'Have respect for older people, someone
who is more experienced than you,
because they can teach you things'*

ALL THINGS ARE POSSIBLE

Anything you want to do, you can do it. You just need to find
the right angle, and usually what that means is understanding
as much as possible about what you want to do. You've heard
the stories about when people started wanting to fly and they
couldn't understand why they couldn't? The first people tried to
fly like a bird, with the flapping of the wings, because that's all
we could think of. But on closer investigation, we realised that
couldn't work for long. Then we discovered we could become
airborne by going against the wind and conquering gravity. So
it goes to show that at first it might seem impossible, but when
you get right down to it, you can get it.

DON'T BEG

Don't beg for anything. It's important because once you start to beg, you put yourself at a very disadvantaged position with whoever you're begging from. You start to beg and it's like you're saying to someone that you want to be fucked all over. Instead you're better off going, 'Now listen, I want to do some business with you, I'm gonna bring this to the table, are you interested in this or that?' And then you do a swap. I like to bring things to the table and I don't expect something for nothing.

THE SOURCE OF THE PAIN MAY NOT BE THE SOURCE OF THE PROBLEM

This goes back to my days of electronics, when I was repairing things. You'd be repairing a mixing desk and there could be a problem at the output stage and you're first inclined to go to where the problem is. Then you investigate further and find that the problem could be at the earlier stages, it could be at the input stage, but unless you isolate it, you don't realise. You can apply it to life in general. It's like in England there's a problem with young guys killing each other and first it could seem like that's where the problem is, but the real problem could be somewhere else that leads to that.

ALWAYS LISTEN TO MIXES IN THE CAR

In the studio everything is big, loud, perfect conditions, but until you compare that condition with another environment, you don't know how suitable it is for general use. When you're driving and you hear something come on incidentally, it can have a different effect from when you're in the studio where everything sounds brilliant. You can't mix in a car, but if you go back and forth, you get a better idea of where you're at.

HELP SOMEONE LESS FORTUNATE THAN YOURSELF

People are people everywhere but it's quite easy for someone who has got a lot and who's been in a comfort zone to think, 'Yeah, I'm alright Jack, I don't care about anyone else.' It's a good thing when you can help someone and give someone a chance. Especially when it's young people or very old people. It's good karma to do that. Being brought up in a Christian home, it's part of what they tell you when you go to Sunday school as a kid in the Caribbean: 'help people less fortunate than yourself.'

EVERYONE IS SPECIAL IN SOME UNIQUE WAY

Not everyone can recognise their special gift. This comes from travelling. When you go to places like Africa, you might find that some people may not be doctors, or lawyers or anything, but you could have an emergency situation and the answer comes from someone who is totally unqualified by Western standards to tell you what to do and by talking to them, you could suddenly get a solution. This person might have nothing at all to do with what you're talking about but they could come up with the most obvious answer, come up with a solution that fits the bill spot on.

DON'T SING WHEN YOUR BELLY IS FULL

Years ago in the studio, we had a session with some guys from South-East London. They were Muslim guys and one of the things they wanted to do before the session was eat, so they had a big spread. We ate and went down to do the session and it couldn't happen. Everyone was starting to yawn and fall asleep. I said, 'Let's call it a day.' From then on, I realised it doesn't make sense to eat before a session. Afterwards is fine, but not before.

HONOUR YOUR MOTHER AND FATHER

This isn't necessarily your flesh mother or your flesh father, but to have that respect for older people, someone who is more experienced than you because they can teach you things. I didn't realise this when I was a young man, only when I was an old man!

YOU'RE NOT YOUNG FOR EVER

The two biggest mistakes that young people make is that they think they're young for ever, and they think older people have always been old. It's only as they go along, they realise. It's the same thing my mum and dad used to tell me and now I'm doing it. We're all young once and always make the mistake of assuming that we'll be young for ever. I'm still pretty hungry to do things. I've still got the hunger to make records that haven't been made before.

IT'S AN ANALOGUE WORLD WE LIVE IN

Digital is noughts and ones, everything drops in a way that it's nought or one. Analogue is a sine wave, it could go anywhere from one to 10. In music and electronics, analogue can be tailored where you can get things like feedback and phasing, and out of that you can create echo and reverb naturally. Analogue is a natural way. Digital is more man-made, and out of digital you can't create effects in the same way. Life is like that. Life is an analogue world. It's an analogue life.

Ezra Furman

Singer-songwriter

'Find the time that's sacred – where you're not trying to change the world or advance your interests, you're just enjoying being alive'

RESPECT WISDOM

I don't really think that human beings have necessarily improved on the way we think. There are ancient ways of thinking, though, that can be proactive to some of our current ways of thinking. Read the Bible, read old poetry and understand that that old, wise and sometimes seemingly illogical stuff goes a lot deeper than you might think. I know that a lot of people scoff at old classics and old ideas of the good, the true and the pure. I'd say don't scoff at that stuff because it's a lot harder than it looks. I hate scoffing. Don't scoff.

PRIZE YOUR INTEGRITY

I'm really into refusing to do the things that everyone is supposed to do. A lot of the time that's things that have a financial incentive, especially for your job or your career. There have been times when I was younger that I'd find myself in front of some corporate logo saying on camera what they've told me to say. Because they were giving me an opportunity to play music, I'd think, 'I'd better do what they tell me.' It's awkward to say, 'I don't want to do that' and maybe you seem like a brat or something, but let go of how you seem when it's a matter of spirit. The integrity of your spirit is to be prized.

TRUST YOUR MORAL INSTINCT

Every person watches the world lower its standards and every person watches their moral instincts be betrayed. It's tempting to just say, 'Well, that's normal and I guess that's fine,' but you just know when something makes you morally sick and when it feels like action is needed. It's a life-long discipline to trust that – you had it since you were a kid, it's something everyone has, what's good and what's right. That instinct has turned out to be more important than the desire to adapt to a crazy world.

TAKE A BREAK

I'm a person who stops working on the seventh day – I don't use electricity or money, I don't travel and I don't work. I don't get paid. It's the best day of my week every single week. You don't have to do that, it's extreme for a lot of people, but the more smartphones develop the more I feel fiercely protective of the time I'm not using them. I see people working all the time – there's almost never a time that they're not working in some way. I think that's dangerous. Find the time that's sacred – where you're not trying to change the world or advance your interests, you're just enjoying being alive.

BE HONEST

This is sometimes a hard one to convince people of but if somebody accidentally pays you a hundred dollars extra and you need that hundred dollars, it is actually worth more for you to tell them, then give it back, than it is to take the hundred bucks that'll get you a place to sleep that night. People remember the honesty and having a habit of honesty is so much more of an asset than some extra money or some advantage you got by lying.

SPEND TIME WITH PEOPLE OLDER THAN YOU

It's been really important to me to spend time with people who are decades older than me. Those relationships are really valuable. There can be some social awkwardness but if you get the chance, if you meet older people and think, 'Maybe I could connect with this person,' go towards them and listen to them, ask them stuff about how they've done it so far. They are gonna say something to you that's different than anyone your age is gonna say. They've got good stories and they can teach you something.

PUSH BACK

If there's something going on in society, or just around you personally, that you oppose, you have to actually oppose it – you can't just not participate. You can't just not be racist, for instance, you have to be anti-racist, you have to push in the other direction. If you're swimming in the other direction, then the current is going to take you. So be against things, be honourably outspoken against the things you think are wrong. Don't just withdraw from them. You're still going to be participating if you don't actively push back.

MAKE YOUR OWN DECISIONS

This is especially valuable to me as an artist, but it's also valuable to anyone deciding the course of their life. I went to a show by the band DeVotchKa when I was 19 and I asked one of the band members if he had any advice for an aspiring artist. The thing that he said that I really remember is, 'everyone thinks they know what you should do, but they don't, only you know what you should do.' And that's always been true. The only thing that powers my life as an artist is that I'm in touch with what I know is good. If I yield to any pressure to do something that doesn't have that spirit of 'this is cool, this is good, this is what I would do,' that's destructive.

BE A CITIZEN

Do stuff that has almost no significance on its own but which you think people should do in general. [In other words] if everyone did it, it'd be better. That's where you can have the most impact, in a way. It might seem like it doesn't matter if you do this ethical thing but it matters more than you think it does.

SAY THANK YOU

Be grateful and say out loud that you're grateful. When someone does something for you or is nice to you, make sure they get thanked – and also be grateful in general. That way of thinking changes your brain, to be saying that you're grateful all the time changes your brain. It makes you happy.

Mark Lanegan

Singer, musician and author

*'It's none of my business what anyone
else thinks of me if I know who I am'*

IT'S GOOD TO BE DIFFERENT

Don't ever let anyone give you shit because you don't fit society's idea of 'normal'. The false sense of security some get by joining the pack of lemmings, who would all don ridiculous red baseball hats originally designed to keep a politician's terrible comb-over in place while he struts around in public, are somehow oblivious of the fact that they will be the first to get fucked over by these shitheads they support. Ignorance is at a place where next week a trip to the doctor's office will get you a chest covered with leeches to fix what ails you. Kids, be brave, be smart and don't buy into the shit you're being shovelled. Know who you are and fearlessly follow your heart. If you are out of step with those around you, embrace it. Look how you want to look, love how and who you want to love, don't take any shit.

GIVE THE GIFT OF HEALING

If you can help one person not feel so alone, you've done a great thing. Music did that for me as a lonely kid.

OWN OR TAKE CARE OF AN ANIMAL

There is nothing like the relationship between an animal and a human. The unconditional love received from a dog or cat, horse or more exotic animal, is like no other. The joy of a puppy tearing circles around the yard, so full of life and fire and the heartache as he grows into an old man and comes to the end of the line. The pain of saying goodbye, the gift of the time you had together and the infinite ways your life is enriched by these experiences.

REMAIN CURIOUS, KEEP LEARNING

I grew up in a small farming/cattle ranching community and, from my earliest memories, I wanted to leave. Through circumstance, drive, and a shit-ton of luck, I have been able to spend the last 35 years travelling for a living. I rarely return to my hometown. I'm of the opinion that when people spend their life in a bubble it breeds fear. Much like Trump's imaginary 'crisis' on the Southern border of the United States, the worldwide hysteria over immigration is driven by fear. I loved Anthony Bourdain. He was an enthusiastic and loyal friend but he was so important because he spent a huge part of his life casually travelling to many places the US government and others vilified, embraced local culture and put a human face on those who the fear-mongers would have us believe are evil. He was a prime example of what love, courage, empathy and compassion look like. Keep learning, keep loving.

EVERY DAY IS A NEW BEGINNING

Every day is an opportunity to create a new future. Don't forget to create your own reality. Know the difference between what you own and what someone else's idea of you is. It's none of my business what anyone else thinks of me if I know who I am.

TRY TO HAVE A JOB YOU ENJOY

Or at least one you can find some satisfaction in. Too many people spend the majority of their lives working a job they hate just to pay the bills. I have been blessed to do something I love for a living, but it gets harder by the year for musicians as the cultural shift in how people get their music has driven many out of the business.

HAVE A MOMENT FOR THE LESS FORTUNATE

Homelessness and poverty are at epic levels in the United States and elsewhere across the globe. Addiction, untreated mental illness, personal tragedy, downsizing businesses, estrangement from – or loss of – family and friends to turn to for help are some of the countless reasons why people can find themselves in this predicament. Whenever I see a homeless person, I remember how close I am to such a situation and how my own experience with homelessness and addiction felt like endlessly climbing Everest – starting over every day, and never reaching the summit. The brutality of living out of doors takes an unbelievable strength of physical and psychic willpower, God forbid by circumstance you ever find yourself there.

LOOK FOR MUSIC OFF THE BEATEN PATH

I will never forget the music that changed my life. Where I grew up most people had no awareness of who Jimi Hendrix was, born just 100 miles away. My saving grace was a small record store run by a hippy who was curious for the new and weird. When he put on the 12-inch single of the Sex Pistols' *Anarchy In The UK*, it changed my life for ever. Later, The Gun Club, Joy Division, The Velvet Underground, Stooges, David Bowie and a hundred other artists continued my quest of discovery for the new, exotic and interesting.

GET YOUR HANDS IN THE DIRT

The Earth is being pillaged and raped to the point where 18.7 million acres a year are being destroyed by deforestation – that breaks down to 27 football fields a minute, an area the size of Switzerland yearly. It is likely too late to turn back the clock on this planet's destruction by the greed of men, but as an individual I try to plant as many trees, flowers and shrubs on my property as possible. There is something meditative about doing some small gesture that gives to the Earth and takes my mind off the futility of my actions.

HAVE A SENSE OF HUMOUR

In this age of technology and social media, people like me who make music are privy to immediate criticism or praise and are able to comment in return just as quickly.

I admit to being guilty of spending too much of my rare down-time taking shots at the low-hanging fruit of the clichéd descriptors, less-than-informed reviewers and the speculators who seem to know the motivation and meaning behind every song lyric. I sometimes find it irresistible to play the curmudgeonly old vampire and show up with a surprise ball-buster at a super-fan's feed on occasion as well. I'm probably the only guy out there who will find faux-fault when someone writes, 'It's his greatest record ever!' Usually the ensuing brief internet conversation ends with me laughing and hopefully my target doing the same.

Mary Wilson

Singer, The Supremes

'Life is a gift because it is a miracle,
so you should respect it'

WORK AT WHAT YOU LIKE TO DO

Not everyone is lucky enough to be rich and famous. Most of us have to work and pay the bills, so try and find what you're good at and like to do. If that's not possible, try several things so if one falls through you have another chance. The Supremes would've gone into higher education if we hadn't had our first Number 1 hit record with [1964's] *Where Did Our Love Go.* Thank God [Motown songwriters] Holland-Dozier-Holland came through with that. But luck is not always on your side, so finding what you're good at is key to being happy as well as making a living.

RESPECT LIFE

To me, life has always been special. As a young child I would always look out our front window and gaze at the clouds and stars in the sky. It was all so beautiful and far away, yet I still felt connected. Even today, at 75 years young, I still look at the trees and flowers and talk to the birds that are outside my window. Life is a gift because it is a miracle, so you should respect it.

CLEAN BEHIND YOUR EARS

This is one of my less philosophical choices, but I like it because it's true! Always keep your gut clean. Meaning . . . I won't explain that one! And also, always clean your ears, because sometimes if you wear glasses and take them off, they smell really horrible because behind the ears it's very dirty. Sometimes people forget to clean behind the ears, especially guys! Now, ladies, I never go to bed with my make-up on. This is crucial because your skin is a beautiful thing so take care of it. And drink lots of water. I live in a desert in Las Vegas so water for me is extremely important to keep my skin looking beautiful.

LEARN FROM YOUR MOTHER

The best advice I've heard from someone else is from my mother, Johnnie Mae. Not so much what she said, but how she lived her life. My mother couldn't read or write, she was poor and uneducated, but she was the best inspiration for me in terms of looking at the world as a beautiful place. I was actually raised by an angel! I don't think I ever saw her mad at anyone.

Maybe she got angry at us kids if we stayed out too late and then we'd get a spanking. Haha!

DREAMS DO COME TRUE

When we were in The Supremes, me, Flo [Ballard] and Diana [Ross] dared to dream. When that dream came true, becoming famous at the age of 20, it was for me like a fairy tale had come true. Even after 60 years, I'm still totally happy about the fame. But I have had things happen to me which could've broken me: my son died in a car accident at the age of 14, I had an abusive marriage, and when Florence died that broke my heart. But, for some reason, I've always been able to get back up, and I think that's thanks to my mom.

ALWAYS LOOK FOR THE TRUTH

The Temptations' song *Beauty Is Only Skin Deep* is a truth that I have learned which also says a lot about seeing the truth in all things. I've always tried to see what was behind something. I would spend hours before falling to sleep analysing something. I ask: 'Who am I? Why did I do some of the things I've done in my life? Do they make me a good or bad person?' I've found that the answer is always be truthful to yourself.

LOVE THY NEIGHBOUR

My intentions have always been to enjoy life and love everyone. However, there have been a few people I have come across in life and no matter how hard I tried, I still could not forgive them for the hurt I felt had been done to me. But as I've grown, I've realised it was not me they were trying to hurt, it was just them being them. People's own hurt can stop them from loving someone. So, love your neighbour, including family and friends, but also learn to love yourself.

GIVE THANKS TO YOUR TEACHERS

I've been blessed to have had so many teachers who have put me on the right track and I give thanks to them all. I was never an A-grade student, but from kindergarten through to high school, I was always chosen to be in the school choir and now I am a famous singer because they gave me the idea. Then, of course, there was Berry Gordy at Motown who took a chance on us. And all our mentors at Motown who said we were diamonds in the rough and that they were just there to shine us up. And shine us up they did!

DON'T LET FAILURE STOP YOU

Failure can stop you in your tracks. Fear is one of those emotions that sets up roadblocks you don't even know are there. I fell off my bicycle when I was nine years old, so I find it hard to ride a bike now. But I am facing things now to overcome old fears which stop me from moving ahead in this life. I'm still working on this.

SLOW DOWN AND SMELL THE ROSES

I've been almost 60 years in showbusiness and I've never thought of retiring. I'm having so much fun writing books and acting so I don't wanna stop. However, I would like to slow down and smell the roses. I've been to all these great exotic countries like Pakistan, Sri Lanka, Japan and China and it would be good to keep travelling to more places. I love to travel, but to do it more as a tourist. So, I'd like to slow down and, obviously, make more money! Haha.

Jason Williamson

Singer, Sleaford Mods

*'Just because you're direct with someone,
it doesn't mean you're a wanker'*

COCAINE, WHY BOTHER?

Anybody who's past the age of 40 and still doing it, it's just a no-no, it's completely wrong. The more I've carried on in the music industry, the more I've realised it's still rife. What the fuck are you doing? It's not aiding and abetting any creativity, it's not making you look cool. The idea of the rock star is gone, it's dead. The idea of this decadent, foppish beautiful soul travelling through the corridors of narcotic-fuelled excess is gone. It just feels like a dated activity.

LET PEOPLE GO

If you're working with people that have come up with you and it feels wrong or the energy's wrong, try and help, try and solve the problem. But if the problem won't go away, if that person or that energy is just completely concrete in its dissonance, just let them go. I used to people-please, and I still do that a lot. But just because you're direct with someone, it doesn't mean you're a fucking wanker. It's for the good of that situation. If people aren't growing with you, let them go.

BE ORIGINAL

Originality is still very achievable. Just because we've had 60 years of popular music, originality is still there. The ways to approach the song is infinite. Messages are quite traditional in the sense that they tend to be stronger and more creatively attractive if they are truthful, or they ape an experience that has been experienced. So it is important to achieve a better level of satisfaction through trying to be original. People know the difference between good and shit music.

IF YOU WANT TO MAKE IT IN MUSIC, DON'T GIVE UP

It's clichéd but it's true: do not give up. You can have periods of rest from it, if it's infuriating to the point that you can't work it, walk away for a while. You will eventually be drawn back into it. If you really love it, if you really want it, you'll be drawn back in. It'll be like somebody's put a lasso around your waist and before you know it, you're doing it again. The main thing is to not give up, to weather it. It's really hard and cheesy but you have to be dead strong.

GO TO THE GYM

If you're feeling down, just go to the gym. If you're gonna spend
£80 on a gram of coke, which a lot of people will, you could
get two personal training lessons out of that, and those personal training lessons will send you miles in front of yourself,
if you concentrate and stick to it. There's nothing wrong with
it, there's nothing to be ashamed about going to the gym and
drinking water after a gig and eating nuts and yoghurt. That's
the way it is. This is the future.

TALK TO YOUR BANDMATES

They're not you, they're different. They have other things that
power their minds. Your annoyance towards them because
they're not you is doomed. It's important to try and understand
them, what makes them why they are the way they are. Get to
know them, get to know them deeply, so then you're prepared
for every day. The main goal here is the songs. Just because
you write great songs with someone doesn't mean you'll get on
brilliantly.

DON'T VOTE CONSERVATIVE

I know it's obvious and people are well aware of this but, simply,
do not vote Conservative. It's such an outdated model of a political party that it shouldn't exist. It just can't keep supporting
a small section of people looking after an even smaller section
of people with all the money, and that's what the Conservative
Party is now. It must run deeper than greed. I think it's down

to the centuries of feudalism, of the aristocracy. It's such an outdated thing. The world can't take this system anymore. Don't vote Conservative. C**ts.

DRINK WATER

Drink loads of water, always. It sorts you right out. Get one of those water filter things, they're fairly cheap – fill it up in the morning, lob it in a beaker, drink that by 10am, keep drinking them throughout the day – you'll feel a lot better. You need water in your body, it just flushes shit out. You piss a lot. I piss about three or four times in the night. It also rinses out your liver and makes it a bit healthier. Or is it your kidneys? I don't know, I'm not a doctor. But drink water.

DON'T COMPROMISE

Compromise is a good idea in an intelligent way, in the sense of becoming part of a team and working alongside people, but don't compromise your creativity. No, no, no. If your creativity is appealing to a lot of people or if you're filling venues with more than 50 people on a consistent basis, you don't compromise. There's no reason why you should have to compromise if you've got a good idea. We've never compromised.

ALLOW FOR OTHERS

We've had to learn a lot about the business side of things and, also, you have to sort out a decent philosophy about it all because a lot of it has no regard for your ego. The more important thing has been dealing with myself, so I have to think, 'I slag a lot of people off, why do I slag them off?' A lot of the time, yeah, I've got a point, but sometimes it's like, 'Have you?' We had to learn about PR, of marketing, of social media, but the most important thing for me has been how to keep your ego at bay and allow for others.

Joe Mount

Frontman and producer, Metronomy

*'Occasionally remind your friends that
you really like them. Just tell them you
love them, there's no shame in it'*

EMBRACE YOUR INNER HIPPY.
BUT NOT ALL OF IT

Think about yourself as part of a planet that is alive. When I say that, I feel like a hippy, but at this point it's important to not be embarrassed by it. The only problem with being a hippy is they make odd aesthetic decisions. Extinction Rebellion – it's a good cause but it's got a shit name. Where I grew up in Totnes, they had a shop called Ethnic Image that sold tie-dye. 'What's ethnic?' 'Oh, you know, stuff from somewhere else.' 'Africa?' 'Dunno, it's just ethnic.'

IT'S NOT ALWAYS A DOG'S LIFE

If you're a dog owner, don't assume everyone likes dogs. For people who are alone I think dogs and cats offer some amazing things, it's just the assumption of pet owners that everyone loves animals. Also, I've got kids, and dogs are scary for kids. A dog will run towards your child and they'll think the dog is about to eat them. The owners will be like, 'Oh he just loves children!' 'What? Have you asked him? How do you know he loves children?'

TELL THEM YOU LOVE THEM

If you have friends that you really like, don't assume they know that. Occasionally remind your friends that you really like them. Just tell them you love them, there's no shame in it. Send a text saying, 'I love you.' They might reply saying, 'I think you sent that to me by mistake.' Then you should reply, 'I didn't, I love you.' Confront them with emotion.

HATS AND WAISTCOATS HAVE NO PLACE ON A STAGE (UNLESS YOU'RE LEONARD COHEN)

I've had this rule for a long time that you should never wear a hat or a waistcoat onstage. It just looks unprofessional. I've never done it, I've only ever worn sunglasses once onstage. True, Leonard Cohen wore a hat but because of his quality, he's the exception to the rule. Even Mumford & Sons have stopped doing it. It's because they realised, you see.

IT'S ABOUT THE JOURNEY, NOT THE DESTINATION

Don't focus on the result, just enjoy the process. There's probably an online self-help person who could put that much better, but there's a lot of things in life that if you don't enjoy the actual act of doing the thing, then you're missing the point. Enjoy the journey. Which is difficult to say when you're on a crap Ryanair flight, but you can apply it to everything.

EAT TOGETHER

Always sit down for dinner. You shouldn't sit in front of the telly. You're allowed to sit in front of the television maybe once a week, but you should otherwise sit down with the people you live with for dinner. It's what separates us from the animals. Pretty much every other European country apart from England places a real importance on the act of sitting down and eating together. People get lazy. I saw a thing in a hotel the other day that said, 'Bring the restaurant to your room.' I was reading it thinking, 'You just mean eating in bed, don't you?'

HAIL TO THE BUS DRIVER

Say thank you to bus drivers. In London, they're making it really hard to say thanks to bus drivers. They're putting them behind Perspex, and you're encouraged to leave by the back door instead of the front. I have memories of growing up in the country and people getting off the bus and going, 'Cheers, driver!' I always enjoy saying thank you to bus drivers. If it was a really, really crowded bus I would maybe give a little wave, because they have to check everyone's off the bus before they do anything with the doors. It's a symbolic thing, I don't know if they've necessarily seen me.

SCHOOL IS COOL

It's important to keep learning about stuff, to take on new information or learn new skills. You get a flurry of education when you're young and then you get a job and just stop. It's good to keep yourself stimulated by things. When I moved to France, I did an intensive language course and it was super cool. When you're at university you might be distracted by girls or parties and stuff but being in an environment where you're just there because you want to learn French was a really fun thing to do.

DON'T BE A SHOW-OFF ON SOCIAL MEDIA

Don't use social media to make people feel jealous. I'm thinking specifically about Instagram. You look and might see someone who'll need to get somewhere, and the only option is to take a private jet, so they take a picture of themselves in front of the aeroplane. The only reason they do it is to make other people feel jealous. The really cool people are taking private jets but they're not bothering to take a picture. No one should feel inferior or superior to anyone else. Instagram can be a fun and positive experience. There's a picture of me having a nosebleed on the Metronomy Instagram? Yeah, I'm living my best life.

TRUST YOUR INSTINCTS

I don't think you should ever have to be persuaded to do something. Your instincts are always right. You might go, 'Oh, OK, I guess you know what you're talking about ...' But no! Sometimes people don't know what they're talking about.

Robert Forster

Singer-songwriter and co-founder of The Go-Betweens

*'The object is to get as much sleep as
you can to feel as good as you can'*

SLEEP IS THE KEY

Without it, you're dead, and with it, you're totally alive. The
object is to get as much sleep as you can to feel as good as you
can. In the music business these days, you need confidence to
go on. If I'm feeling brittle or like I'm not at full strength, I tend
to get a bit shaky. I need nine hours, which I know is going to
sound like an astonishing amount. When I get that, which I do
most days, I wake up good and I'm enthusiastic about what I'm
about to do. It's a great basis for the day.

DRIVE SLOWLY

Brisbane, where I live, is very much a car town. It's like Los
Angeles, so you spend a lot of time in the car and you have

people two inches from your bumper and there's people dodging in and out, risking your life and others, and I just look and think, 'Why are these people doing that?' It's not as if they're off to paint the Sistine Chapel or they've got a lunch date with Oscar Wilde. There can't be anything that important to create so much danger. I drive slowly, and there's a little bit of pleasure because you can actually see the steam coming out of people's ears in the cars behind you.

VALUE FRUIT

When I look at the design and beauty of an apple or an orange, its real worth for something as beautiful and as neat as that would be, like, a hundred quid. That's what an apple should cost because it's so perfect. But we get them for 50p! I've been an avid fruit-eater my whole life. Fruit is a great luxury, fruit's a great cheap luxury. When I go past a fruit stand, it's like passing an art gallery. I find it spectacular. And we're not even talking about the health benefits, we're just talking about apples and pears. We're not even talking about the pineapple or the watermelon, which are like drug-inducing fruits. The beauty and the cheapness of fruit is very overlooked.

JULIE ANDREWS INVENTED FOLK ROCK

A lot of people think The Byrds invented folk rock when they recorded *Mr Tambourine Man* in the middle of 1965. But if you look at Julie Andrews in *The Sound Of Music*, there's a whole 1962/63 Greenwich Village vibe that's coming off her. There's a scene in the film where she's running through a shaded grove with the children and they're singing *Do-Re-Mi* and she has the gingham dress and the androgynous hair. There's something about that image that to me is one of the great four or five images of the '60s. To me, that's where folk rock starts, and everything else comes after Julie, after *Do-Re-Mi*, after that moment in the grove.

SHARE LOST TREASURE

As a singer-songwriter, there's three albums that are very special to me. One of them is *Blood On The Tracks* by Bob Dylan, the next one is *Astral Weeks* by Van Morrison and the third is Guy Clark's *Old No.1*. They're very different but all as good as each other and all pinnacle achievements in singer-songwriting. *Old No.1* is chronically under-appreciated. I want everyone to hear it. I'm always one for sharing these things, that they get their recognition.

FREQUENT BOOKSHOPS

You don't even have to buy a book there. It's the same with libraries: it's the quality that books have to calm people down. I sit there, surrounded by tables and shelves with books on, and naturally feel better. It's different to a record shop. For a start, you've got the almost silence. Occasionally I've been in a bookshop and they've played something at low volume – that's been really nice. To walk out of a busy city and into a bookshop is always a good thing, it's good for your blood pressure if nothing else.

ONLY DO SOCIAL MEDIA IF YOU WANT TO

There are two kinds of people: those who feel comfortable with social media and those who don't. And those people were like that before social media was invented. Social media is suitable to people who are gregarious and want to connect with friends and family. But there's another group of people who are quieter, yet have an expectation that they should join in. People should have the confidence to keep their involvement to whatever level they want.

BEWARE OF DENIM

When I look at photos of Led Zeppelin or rock groups of that era, there's a lot of denim and centre-parted long hair and grit. To me, [US folk trio] Peter, Paul And Mary are a better-looking band than Led Zeppelin. Two guys with goatee beards and sharp black suits and, in the middle of them, Mary Travers with her fringe across the brow, the blonde hair and great voice. That's a great look for a band. I get a vibe off that that I don't get from a late-'60s rock band.

BE CURIOUS

This links back to getting enough sleep. If you've got enough sleep, you've got the energy to be curious. I think being curious spills over into life. Life is like detective work. You've got to follow leads, things come along that you don't expect, and the amount of knowledge you've got helps you. And I don't mean the big questions about life, it could be reading the ingredients list on a product in the supermarket. It's just information-gathering, but it's a powerful thing to have.

DRUGS ARE OVERRATED

I think everyone knows that drugs are bad, so I think another angle has to be taken. Drugs are overrated as a point of enjoyment. As a Saturday night thrill, drugs aren't as good as they're made out to be. It's an unknown substance that you're taking and paying hefty money for. Is it worth it?

Jenny Lewis

Singer-songwriter

'There's nothing worse than hanging out with someone and they roll over in bed to check their Instagram DMs'

DRINK MORE WATER

I've always disliked water, which is a really funny thing because our bodies are about 60 per cent water so to not like it is to not like yourself. Johnny [Rice, singer-songwriter], when we were together for 12 years, was a great encourager of hydration, but we broke up three years ago now so I'm really fucking dehydrated! But you find coping mechanisms: Bill Murray has this technique of putting champagne over ice and when it melts you get your water intake. I also enjoy a tequila soda, is that considered water?

ALWAYS RETURN THE SHOPPING CART

It's the little things in life that feel insignificant, but really only take a minute to make someone else's life a little easier. And I've witnessed people not returning the shopping cart and I judge them. Even if it's raining, return the fucking shopping cart!

WORK ON BECOMING A BETTER LISTENER

Nobody likes a one-sided rant. And if you're listening to your friend on the phone who's telling you a story, be sure to say 'Uh-huh' or 'Yes' or 'Hmm' every now and then because otherwise they'll think either you're not engaged or not there. This also applies to listening to new music: try to listen to the whole song or LP all the way through. Your inclination is to skip, but you should always give it a fair shot.

MAKE EYE CONTACT/DON'T MAKE EYE CONTACT

Obviously, eye contact is very important. I've dated a couple of people who don't make eye contact and that is a red flag. When I'm out in the world, meeting people, or singing onstage, I want to connect, and making eye contact is a really powerful thing. You feel a person's soul and energy when you look into their eyes. Conversely, not making eye contact can also be a good thing. Apparently when women are having sex and making eye contact, they release a bonding chemical in their brains. Men also release this chemical, however alcohol neutralises it. So, my advice for single women who are sexually active and safe: if you don't want to feel so bonded to your partner, don't make eye contact while you're having sex. Imagine dating a narcoleptic? That takes it to a whole other level!

SONGWRITING IS NOT THERAPY

You can purge all you like and write about the demons but in no way is that ample exorcising. Also get some advice and guidance from a professional if need be. I beg you.

BELIEVE PEOPLE WHEN THEY TELL YOU WHO THEY ARE

If someone tells you that they have no moral compass, believe them. We like to think people are up for changing, even when they show no signs of changing. I believe in growth, but I don't know if I believe in a fundamental, philosophical change. I think people are pretty much who they are, so if they say, 'Beware, stay away, I'm an asshole', it's probably a good idea to do that.

THE ROAD NARROWS

This one really sucks. The things that used to distract us – alcohol, drugs, relationships, sex – kind of stop working in the same way as you get older. Your karmic path, or journey, will still be present but when it comes down to it, it's just you, so wherever you go is where you are. Sure, you can go off in different directions, but all paths will eventually lead back to you and the way you feel about yourself. It's a lot easier to think that booze and pills do the trick, but I think if you ask anyone it's hard work that does it, and it's hard for a reason.

GET 20 MINUTES OF DIRECT SUNLIGHT EVERY DAY

This is a big one for me. Make sure you do this on as much exposed skin as possible and with no sunblock. And it's important to do this before 11am and after 4pm when the UV rays aren't so strong. I think we're running around in this world vitamin D-depleted and a little bit of sunlight on your bod really makes you feel better and will improve your mental state too. So put your palms up to the sun and give it a high-five. I'm a Californian, hence my cheery disposition!

KEEP THE CELLPHONE OUT OF THE BEDROOM

I can't say I always adhere to this rule, because I really do like to wake up and check the news on Twitter, which is a terrible habit. But when I keep the phone in the kitchen, I sleep through the night and feel so much better. Also, if the phone's out of the bedroom, it prevents sneaky photos or videos. There's nothing worse than hanging out with someone and they roll over in bed to check their Instagram DMs.

WINE AND WEED IS ALL YOU NEED

If you've got to check out a little bit, keep it safe with a little grass and a Beaujolais. They're natural, man! I mean, I've seen people spiral out on marijuana, however it is a relatively safe substance. Pharmaceuticals are a slippery slope – I've seen people come off psych meds and Valium and it's not a pretty sight. But be careful about mixing wine and weed, a couple of times I've woken up on the ladies' room floor in a club in Silverlake with like four girls above me going. 'Are you OK?' I'm like, 'I just smoked a joint and had a glass of wine, what happened?!'

Robyn

Producer and synth-pop star

*'Things take time and that's good. If they
don't, something is probably a little fishy'*

LEARN TO CHILL OUT

I think the best piece of advice I've ever been given was by a
very good friend of mine who told me just to chill out. When
I learned to chill out things became a lot easier for me. Just
generally in life things become much more pleasant if you take
it a little bit more easy. I can be quite, you know, intense and
impatient. So maybe I just take a couple of extra breaths and
that usually does the trick. It's all about trying to be present
and to not stress.

TAKE A TRIP

My parents had an independent theatre company as I was growing up and I think being around them, watching them working

and collaborating, plus doing a lot of travelling, probably had an influence on me. When I was younger, I think I'd had enough of the travelling, I just wanted my family to be normal, but now that I'm older I'm happy they took me along. Travelling opens your mind. Seeing things for the first time makes me wake up, I really enjoy what it does to my brain.

WORK THE WAY YOU WANT

I started writing my new album [*Honey*] in 2014 and the way I approached making it this time around was very different to how I worked before. It was different in the sense that I worked with a lot of new people, mostly Joseph Mount [of Metronomy] who was the main producer of the album, and I think that in itself, working with a new person, made things different. But I also spent a lot of time on my own preparing the album, so I think the way that I approached my song writing was different too.

ALL GOOD THINGS COME TO THOSE WHO WAIT

I was definitely nervous thinking that eight years was a long time for my fans to wait for a new album. But once I had music and had the album ready, it didn't feel stressful anymore because the excitement of sharing the music takes over. When you've taken time to get it right and the music is ready, it's not stressful anymore. But before I knew what I was going to do, it could feel quite stressful, but I kind of learned how to deal with it during the making of this record.

GET A FULL NIGHT'S SLEEP

In the last year or two I've realised that my biggest source of inspiration is sleep. I had a long period when I was really sad and I didn't sleep much, and I think I just realised how important it is to sleep. When you don't sleep, everything feels dull and my brain feels one-dimensional. Life just gets boring. I like how free I feel when I'm not tired.

AVOID RESPECTING TECHNOLOGY TOO MUCH

The machines and software I use in the studio are supposed to help me do what I want, not the other way around. You don't have to use them in the way you've heard others use them, unless it's something you like and want to imitate. You can do what you want. If you have something in mind that you are feeling, then do it – even if it seems silly. If there's a piece of tech that you are interested in, even if it's not 'within your field' of music, then try it anyway. The demos I made for this album sound way different than what ended up on the record.

DON'T SMOKE CIGARETTES

It's really hard to stop and they don't even make you high.

TRY NOT TO RUSH THINGS

A few years ago, before I started Konichiwa Records, I realised that people don't make time to understand what they are doing and whether it works or not. I felt like I was putting in so much work, and then someone else would come in and not care about it the way I did. Many people don't care about the things they do, or why things are the way they are. I appreciate that when things are complex, they are often more interesting. I also like to learn about what I'm doing so I can make and do things that are meaningful. Things take time and that's good. If they don't, something is probably a little fishy.

RULES ARE FOR FOOLS

There are no rules in fashion – that would be really bad. When people ask me for fashion tips I don't want to say anything, I feel uncomfortable giving advice like this. I never even think about it – fashion advice is just stupid.

FIND TIME TO BE HAPPY

I don't even know what happy means, but I guess that I'm at my happiest when I have time. Time for my friends and my family, time to not do much but just be with the people I love. You never know how much time you'll have so better enjoy it while you can.

Riz Ahmed

Actor and rapper

*'I really believe that everything humans
do is either drawn by fear or love'*

GET OUT OF YOUR OWN WAY

Sometimes you're exhausted and you just need to do nothing.
I have lulls that are a bit less hectic and I think that's healthy. I
think of it less as, 'Oh shit! The muse has abandoned me!' and
a bit more like, 'OK, cool, your brain and your mind and your
body need some space to be able to get back into a receptive
space.' The best thing you can do is get out of your own way.
That's a big block creatively, that's a big block in life, trying to
hold onto things and drag them this way, drag them that way.
Yes, have a clear intention, yes, work towards those goals, but
try and eliminate yourself from the equation. Try and eliminate
your own fears, your own ego.

DON'T BE DRAWN INTO THE CYCLE OF BAD VIBES

I try and see where people are coming from. Even if someone is being snaky, or someone's being fake, or someone's being really negative, or someone's being really aggressive, now I think I'm a bit older, I think, 'OK, that person's in some pain, man, that person's afraid.' I really believe that everything humans do is either drawn by fear or love. Really, nine times out of ten, when someone is coming from that negative place, that negative energy is coming from a place of fear. Does it mean it's my problem to absorb it and to fix it for them? No, but at least I can try and be a bit more kind in how I receive it and not judge them back and get into a dirty cycle of bad vibes.

YOU DON'T HAVE CONTROL

The hardest thing I've ever had to do is jump off a cliff. I did it in Jamaica, to try and get over my fear of jumping off cliffs. I went through this waterfall and there was a cliff and I was like, 'Ah, man, that's so scary.' My legs froze up, and I was like, 'You know what, man, you're scared of jumping off this cos you think you'll lose control when you jump.' The reality is, when you jump, you don't have any fucking control at any point. You think you've got control of your life, nah, you don't have any control over anything, so lean into it.

DON'T SELL YOURSELF SHORT

I was told this by [bhangra artist] Bally Jagpal backstage at a daytime rave in 1996. Every time you think, 'Fuck, I can't do this,' think, 'Well, maybe I can.' If you keep on going, keep challenging yourself, you keep making new leaps. A big leap for me initially was putting out [2006 single] *Post 9/11 Blues*. It was a way of turning feelings of negativity into something that could be cathartic for people, understanding that those dark feelings aren't things you have to push aside to be creative, they are things you can harness.

USE WHAT YOU'VE GOT

I was the youngest kid in a noisy house full of playful, big personalities. My earliest shit that I used to do was a Prince Charles impression, cos I had big ears. You've gotta use what you've got. I don't know if you ever go, 'Yes! I can do this really well!' That's not how I think of it. I think, 'OK, I like doing this, I think I want to do this, how can I keep getting better at doing it?'

SPEND TIME WITH YOUR FAMILY

My biggest regret is not spending more time with family. If you're living a life that's not particularly settled and you're always on the move, there are sacrifices in terms of stability for some of your personal relationships. Family is something you constantly discover as you get older. There's something unconditional, something that's an implicit common ground and understanding, and even though family often brings a lot of expectation and frustration and can bring conflict, the ability to try and work through those are what life's about.

CELEBRATE LONDON'S MULTICULTURALISM

London is the most multicultural city in the world. I just walked through Burgess Park [near Camberwell] and there's a group of Polish dudes all fishing, there's a group of old Moroccan uncles blazing some hash, there's random Congolese dudes comparing their bikes, it's the world in one city.

FIND YOUR FIX

I'm happiest performing onstage. You get that instant connection with a massive group of people, when they're all locked in with you, that feeling of transcending your singular individual experience and connecting with a larger group of people. That's a spiritual experience. You can feel it when you're raving. You can feel it when you're performing, and the crowd are locked in. You can find it in religion. People find it in different ways. You can find it in the army. It's that whole feeling of when the drop of water reaches the ocean. Connecting to that group experience. It expands your sense of who you are.

KEEP FACING FORWARD

I rarely sit back and take stock and go, 'Yes! You're good! You can do this; you can do this.' It's much more like, 'Ah, shit, this is another thing I can work on.' And you get obsessed with that.

It's a never-ending thing you're always chasing. I very rarely stop and take stock, it's always forward-facing on the next thing you can do and the next thing you can improve on.

THE REAL YOU IS CONSTANTLY SHIFTING

I used to think that acting and music were more different, now I realise they are more the same. I used to think they were more different cos one was the real me and the other thing was being other people, but now I feel like, even the idea of the real you is constantly shifting. The beat tells you who you are in that moment – whatever you've read that morning, whoever you've spoken to the night before, shapes who you are. It's the same with acting, the environment and the people you're acting opposite shape who you are. Creatively, they're both about being open to the moment, trusting your gut and jumping.

Tom Morello

Guitarist, Rage Against The Machine

'I realised at a young age that when it came to certain ethical matters, my compass was very different'

DON'T WORRY ABOUT YOUR GUITAR TONE

This is anathema to guitar players who slavishly work away at particular tones. I tried for years to find this magical tone that was in my head and I finally just gave up and played with the crappy tone I had and said, 'I'm never gonna worry about it another day in my life, I'm just gonna make music that sounds good with the tone I've got' and that ended up being Rage Against The Machine.

CONFRONT INJUSTICE AT EVERY TURN

This was something that was embedded in me by my mom when I was four years old. Some older kid at day-care was doing some racial name-calling at me every day and I was crying, and my mom said, 'you're the one who has to confront it.' She gave me some choice words to say back, rolled my little brown hand into a fist and said, 'go back there and give 'em hell.' The kid was N-wording me and I called him whatever my mom had said, a big fight broke out and eventually when the supervisor came over and sussed it all out, the kid was taken over to the sink and had his mouth washed out with soap. Whether you see someone bullying on the playgrounds, or a boss being abusive at work, or a government being abusive to the people in it or under it, it's important to confront it.

PRACTICE MAKES PERFECT

This was advice given to me by a more advanced guitar player in high school and I took it as biblical script. I practised every day and I realised the tide of my ability was rising because of that. Eventually it was eight hours a day, every day, without fail. It was a commitment to a goal that you can extrapolate. You can do that in any endeavour and achieve real results.

ALL THE WORLD IS A LITTLE WEIRD

My grandmother told me this. There was some kid doing something peculiar and she pointed out that I had some peculiar faculties myself! I thought, 'You're right'. Celebrating the differences and the weirdness in others and ourselves is better than casting aspersions and condemning people for standing out.

FORGIVE OTHERS, AND YOURSELF

In forgiving others, you can become free and clean to move forward and, in forgiving yourself, you're able to open new doors to new experiences. Wayne Kramer of the mighty MC5 gave me great advice. He'd taken me to some charity event and I just behaved awfully to the host. Afterwards I was beating myself up and he said, 'It's OK to make mistakes, everybody makes 'em and you're a good person.' I felt absolved in some way. Forgiving myself was key to moving forward.

BELIEVE IN WHAT YOU DO

I didn't move to Hollywood to become a political firebrand, I moved to Hollywood to become a rock star. I was a neophyte from Smalltown, Illinois. I got in a band and the record company said to do this, and the producer said to do that, and a lot of it didn't feel right, but I thought, 'They're the experts, they must know best'. After that band was dropped from the label, I made a solemn vow to myself to never play music I didn't believe in. I've stuck to that from that day to this.

QUESTION EVERYTHING

I realised at a very young age that when it came to certain ethical matters, my compass was very different from the textbook I was reading, or the way the teacher was describing the Cold War, stuff like that. I began questioning out loud in class and writing letters to the editor of newspapers. When I found that I could win an argument with a teacher, it made me go, 'Hold on, maybe the guy on the news is no smarter than this guy, or has a perspective that is equally invalid.' That really began a lifetime of questioning everything.

LIFE MATTERS ALL OVER THE WORLD

We just had the yearly 9/11 mourning here in the States, very rightly memorialising the civilians who'd been killed, and it's a reminder of how good Americans can be and how empathetic they can feel. Too often, that empathy ends at the border and when it comes to American drones killing people overseas, we turn a blind eye, we don't count the dead, we don't know their names. That is at the core of a lot of evil in the world: viewing people, who don't look like you or come from where you are, as less deserving of empathy.

YOU ARE NOT WHAT YOU OWN

In this rabid consumer culture, the intrinsic worth of a person is not tied up in their material possessions at all. I know some very wealthy people who have helicopters, and who have sadness and sickness in their souls, and I've known people who are hopeless drug addicts or prostitutes who had hearts of gold and were deeply worthwhile humans.

YOU ARE AN AGENT OF HISTORY

The world changes when somebody changes it and injustice stops when somebody stops it. The people who've changed the world in the past have no more power or courage or intelligence than the people reading this now. You can choose to stay on the side-lines with your head in a hole like an ostrich, or you can join the countless others who have stood up in their place and time to create a more just and humane planet.

Bugzy Malone

Rapper

'Just because the beginning looks a little bit dark you can still learn how to do anything that you want in life. Don't be afraid to aim big'

HAVE A USP

As a kid I was called Bugz. It wasn't the coolest nickname in the world. In fact, a lot of people would say, 'Are you named after Bugs Bunny?' But in the end, because the name was attached to me, the name became cool, know what I mean? It's probably the same with my Mancunian accent. When people first heard me, they might've thought, 'What's his accent?' But because there's never been a Manchester grime MC before me that's been successful, my accent worked in my favour. I've made it cool, so now it's my USP.

PUT THINGS INTO PERSPECTIVE

When I was in prison [aged 16] I put my situation into perspective. We all have personal perspectives and mine was, 'I'm young, just a kid, can I afford to waste my time in here?' So I started writing lyrics properly for the first time, and taught myself how to be obedient and disciplined. But I think a lot of people who get into that situation think, 'Oh, I've messed my life up, nothing good is gonna come from this.' So, yeah, it gave me perspective, which kept me positive. My advice to anyone young growing up in the same difficult situation as me is: aim to escape it, rather than trying to handle it. Just because the beginning looks a little bit dark you can still learn how to do anything that you want in life. Don't be afraid to aim big.

GET THE BALANCE RIGHT

There's a balance to everything and you need to find it. For example, if you eat too healthily every day, then eventually you're just going to be craving sweets so much that's all you're gonna eat all the time. So, find a balance between healthy and unhealthy. Don't overdo either. I find the balance in stages – I might be balanced for three months and I might get my best work done in that time, but fame is quite unbalancing, so I might lose it for a couple weeks until I find it again.

BE STRICT ON YOURSELF

In order to get the things done that you want to do in life, you have to be strict on yourself. So you need to be disciplined, in your work and when you're relaxing. Focus on yourself and don't worry about other people. Be strong-minded and don't fear going it alone. I feel like, even though you've got friends and family, you're still here alone, so in a lot of situations you have to be by yourself. You can't just rely on other people.

LOOK BEYOND FOR INSPIRATION

One of my favourite films of all time is *Kill Bill*. I think that when you take into consideration that someone wrote that film, somebody else cast the actors, sourced the locations, did the art-work, put it all together into this finished package, I think that's just mind-blowing. I was a creator on a low level when I first saw that film a few years ago, and I recognised *Kill Bill* is a creation on a high level. I found it inspirational, so I started to look into Quentin Tarantino, to see if there was any rhythm to the way he worked. I direct my own videos as well, so I'm always trying to come up with fresh ways to put my points across. I find watching Tarantino videos more inspiring than listening to other grime artists. I try to look outside of my field for inspiration.

TELL YOUR STORY

I'm a creative. When I got an opportunity to do Fire In The Booth [performing track *0161* on the 2015 Radio 1Xtra session, receiving 12 million views], rather than just going in there and spitting lyrics about anything, I told my story, knowing that I was going to be exposed to a bigger audience. It was quite a rounded-off package – all the good, bad and ugly. I was professional so I was invited back.

LEARN TO VISUALISE

I read a book called *The Secret* [Rhonda Byrne, 2006] about the laws of attraction and it basically tells you to visualise what it is you want, or where you see things going. Keep a positive attitude, stay focused and eventually it kind of materialises.

MASTER A CRAFT

I believe that once you become a master of a craft, then anything else you want in life will drop into place. I still do boxing training and how often I go varies from week to week, so I'm kind of still climbing the ladder. Boxing is all about movement, so you're kind of getting in touch with your body. It's like meditation.

KEEP IT FRESH

With music I'm always trying to find different metaphors to get points across. Those metaphors can be cars, sport, food, the streets ... I'm always looking for different ones to keep it fresh. I'm kind of speaking in code. If you know what I'm talking about, you know. If you don't know what I'm talking about, you'll think I'm talking about actual things. When I used Oasis lyrics [*Memory Lane* borrows from *Wonderwall*] that was different, I was paying homage to the originals. When I supported Liam [at Lancashire County Cricket Club last month] it was epic. It was a really well put-together show. I really enjoyed it.

ALWAYS THINK BIG

Don't be afraid to be ambitious and think big and outside of the box. My success is down to a combination of all these things I've just mentioned. Stay focused, healthy and positive.

Slaves

Punk duo

'All of your arguments could evaporate into thin air if you just said you were wrong and take it on the chin'

EVERYONE DESERVES A THIRD CHANCE

Laurie Vincent: Anyone can have a bad day, so you should give everyone two chances.

Isaac Holman: At least. It's very easy to judge someone on your first encounter with them. I bet I've been a dick to people the first time I've met them if I was having a shit day.

LV: The kind of industry we're in, tempers and emotions run high so you should give people two chances and, if you can stretch to it, three. I've met some horrible people on first encounter that have actually just been having a bad time.

KNOW WHEN TO CALL IT A NIGHT

IH: Don't go to the after-party. You'll embarrass yourself and you'll regret it in the morning. I'm so guilty of chasing the night. When you notice it's eight in the morning and you're round someone's house you don't know, talking shit about their childhood and making plans to go to the Science Museum.

LV: I've heard you do that so many times.

IH: I actually did try and go to the Science Museum on a comedown once and it was not fun at all. It was horrible. Don't ever go to the Science Museum on a comedown, that's also a good rule.

KILL WITH KINDNESS

LV: Be nice to everyone. You can really convert someone by not lowering yourself to their grumpiness.

IH: Always be nice, you'll feel a lot better for it. It's not good for anyone if you just give it back.

DON'T FEAR THE Y-FRONT

LV: Try out Y-fronts. So many of you will realise that they're much more comfortable than you think. I'm not saying that they're for everyone, but just try them. It's not a good look picking your pants out of your arse in public and Y-fronts don't give you a wedgie because they go into the cracks so don't ride up. I made the move a couple of years ago. We started wearing the H&M David Beckham range. They're not as attractive when you're not wearing trousers, admittedly.

SATISFY YOUR CRAVINGS

LV: When you're ordering in a restaurant you should go with your first instinct, then at least you've explored that avenue. You should always satisfy the craving because you could walk out of that restaurant and get hit by a bus.

IH: Satisfy your needs. And have pudding. There's always space for pudding.

LV: Pudding makes life better.

IH: I fucking love pudding so much.

CREASED IS NOT THE WORD

IH: When you play a gig, always, always make sure the venue has an iron. I get really funny about that. If they haven't got one, I'll go and buy one.

LV: Just don't go out with creased trousers or a creased shirt on. No one is going to respect you.

IH: I love ironing. I get offstage sometimes and do some ironing, it calms me down.

LV: You've got to have a high-quality iron. You're going to buy it twice if you buy a shit one. It's got to be a big name, like Braun.

ADMIT WHEN YOU'RE WRONG

LV: So many arguments stem from people who can't say they're wrong, even if they know they are. We're programmed to be stubborn. All of your arguments could evaporate into thin air if you just said you were wrong and take it on the chin.

IH: I don't think we've ever had a flat-out row. Maybe one or two.

LV: I stopped talking to Isaac once.

IH: It lasted for two days. We had a little bicker in ASDA and it got out of hand.

LV: I didn't like the way that Isaac talked to me and went, 'That's it! I've put up with a lot of shit over the years and now you've pushed me one step too far!' It can be quite cathartic.

OPEN ALL BOXES, EXHAUST ALL AVENUES

LV: It's important that you try lots of things out. For example, you could always not release a piece of music, but you might as well write it first. It's important to be open-minded and try things out.

IH: It applies to anything: clothes, people . . . sauces.

DON'T COMPARE YOURSELF TO OTHERS

LV: I spent too long looking at other people and wanting to look like them. I spent my teens wearing skinny jeans which look great on tall, skinny people but I've got fucking monster legs.

IH: We're quite chunky so we need a wider trouser. Even slim is too tight. Levi's 511, woah, I can't even get them on. People might see this rule and think we're going to be deep but we're just talking about trousers.

FULLY COMMIT

LV: People ask us if we have any advice for young bands and I think that full commitment is the most important thing ever. Don't say, 'We're going to start a band and we're going to try it, but I can't do Sunday because I've got my nan's 80th.' If you want to be successful you've got to give up everything else. Everything else is less important.

Robin Pecknold

Fleet Foxes frontman

*'Having a clear conscience is
more valuable than gold'*

KEEP A BEGINNER'S MINDSET

I try to keep in mind the thought that there is no arriving at any destination. I try to stay in the mindset of a beginner as much as I can, or do things that I'm not good at, or try to learn new things, to not feel like I've come to any destination, because I feel like that's when someone would lose enthusiasm or passion or a necessity to keep working on things. There's probably some Hallmark card that most of my Commandments are on, but this one's important for sure.

DON'T CUT CORNERS

Integrity is how you do something that people won't see or reward you for. You know if you got the details right, or if you've sweated the details. Most stuff I really admire feels like it was made without cutting any corners. It doesn't always necessarily pay dividends, but I feel like the really great songwriters and melody writers go the extra mile. It does pay off in personal satisfaction.

WORK ON YOUR LIFE

Something I've thought about a lot over the last few years is the Chekhov quote, 'If you want to work on your art, work on your life.' It's trying to keep in mind that the best way forward creatively in arts isn't necessarily sitting down with a guitar and trying to work on something. Exposing yourself to different things, artistic or otherwise, and living a full life and having your work be the fruit of that, rather than it being the only thing that's there.

STEAL THE PROCESS, NOT THE PRODUCT

Try and learn how someone made something but don't copy the thing that they've made. If you copy what someone did, then you won't be able to sleep at night. But if you learn the lesson from them as an artist/person, and just how they approached their problem or what they've made, there's a lot to learn from that without copying the thing itself. You can learn from people in all walks of life and then apply it to what you do yourself.

CALL YOUR FAMILY

I try and remember this as much as I can on tour. Sometimes it's really hard to connect with my family and I try and make more of an effort at it, because I end up missing them a lot when I'm gone. When I'm home we see each other a lot – we're a really close family and we all support each other, and we all get along. We're all pretty independent, so it's a good dynamic.

AVOID VAMPIRES

Don't waste time on things or people that drain your life force. The vampires can come in many different shapes and sizes, and it's important to recognise that and be selective about who you spend your time with. Try to put yourself in situations that make you feel good. Sometimes I didn't see any other way around it, but now I'm more selective or conscious of that kind of thing.

VALUE A CLEAR CONSCIENCE

Having a clear conscience is more valuable than gold. At the end of the day, if you can sleep soundly and you don't hate yourself, then that's so much more valuable than any material or social gain that you might be lusting after.

SURF'S UP

Everyone should surf if they can, make the effort whenever they're close to the water. I first surfed about six years ago and it's great. It's helped me psychologically in so many ways. It's sort of impossible, and sometimes you almost drown, but then you float back up. It's a very quick way towards failing in a good way and staying humble, and in touch with your mortality.

MOODY DOESN'T MEAN SERIOUS, HAPPY DOESN'T MEAN FRIVOLOUS

I think for a long time I was putting moody music with serious music, and happy music with frivolous music, and I don't really think that's the case anymore. I think that that's a false equivalence. Michael Jackson's music is as serious as Will Oldham's, and there's something serious about having a need to want to bring people joy and bring them together. Right now, I'm interested in how to make joyous music that's also serious.

ACT FROM A PLACE OF LOVE, NOT FEAR

There's the Talking Heads line, 'Never for money, always for love' from *This Must Be The Place (Naive Melody)*. You can be afraid for your survival, so you do something for money, or you can do the exact same thing because you love that thing. I just try and keep an open mind as much as possible, like: 'Am I doing this because I love it? Or am I doing this because I'm afraid of something?' Try to chase things and go after them with passion, rather than being in a survival mindset or a state of constant fear of losing something.

Acknowledgements

With thanks to the following contributors:

Matt Allen, Chris Catchpole, Niall Doherty, Tom Doyle, Dave Everley, George Garner, Simon McEwen, Craig McLean, Ben Mitchell, Matt Mason, Michael Odell, Sylvia Patterson, Andrew Perry, Paul Stokes.